Moral Principles and Medical Practice

The Basis of Medical Jurisprudence

Charles Coppens

LECTURE I.
INTRODUCTORY—THE FOUNDATION OF JURISPRUDENCE.

Gentlemen:—1. When I thoughtfully consider the subject on which I am to address you in this course of lectures, i.e., Medical Jurisprudence, I am deeply impressed with the dignity and the importance of the matter.

The study of medicine is one of the noblest pursuits to which human talent can be devoted. It is as far superior to geology, botany, entomology, zoölogy, and a score of kindred sciences as its subject, the body of man, the visible lord of the creation, is superior to the subject of all other physical sciences, which do so much honor to the power of the human mind; astronomy, which explores the vast realms of space, traces the courses and weighs the bulks of its mighty orbs; chemistry, which analyzes the minutest atoms of matter; physics, which discovers the properties, and mechanics, which utilizes the powers of an endless variety of bodies—all these noble sciences together are of less service to man than that study which directly promotes the welfare of his own structure, guards his very life, fosters the vigor of his youth, promotes the physical and mental, aye, even the moral, powers of his manhood, sustains his failing strength, restores his shattered health, preserves the integrity of his aging faculties, and throughout his whole career supplies those conditions without which both enjoyment and utility of life would be impossible.

The physician, indeed, is one of the most highly valued benefactors of mankind. Therefore he has ever been held in honor among his fellow-men;

by barbarous tribes he is looked upon as a connecting link between the visible and the invisible world; in the most civilized communities, from the time of Hippocrates, the father of medicine, to the present day, he has been held in deeper veneration than the members of almost any other profession; even in the sacred oracles of Revelation his office is spoken of with the highest commendation: "Honor the physician," writes the inspired penman, "for the need thou hast of him; for the Most High hath created him. The skill of the physician shall lift up his head, and in the sight of great men he shall be praised. The Most High has created medicines out of the earth, and a wise man shall not abhor them. The virtue of these things is come to the knowledge of men, and the Most High has given knowledge to men, that He may be honored in His wonders. By these He shall cure and shall allay their pains, and of these the apothecary shall make sweet confections, and shall make up ointments of health, and of His works there shall be no end." (Ecclus. xxxiii. 1–7).

2. It is well to remind you thus, gentlemen, at the opening of this new year of studies, of the excellence of your intended profession; for you cannot help seeing that a science so noble should be studied for a noble purpose. In this age of utilitarianism, it is, alas! too common an evil that the most excellent objects are coveted exclusively for lower purposes. True, no one can find fault with a physician for making his profession, no matter how exalted, a means of earning an honest livelihood and a decent competency; but to ambition this career solely for its pecuniary remuneration would be to degrade one of the most sublime vocations to which man may aspire. There is unfortunately too much of this spirit abroad in our day. There are too many who talk and act as if the one highest and worthiest ambition of life were to make as large a fortune in as short a time and in as easy a way as possible. If this spirit of utilitarianism should become universal, the sad consequence of it to our civilization would be incalculable. Fancy what would become of the virtue of patriotism if

officers and men had no higher ambition than to make money! As a patriotic army is the strongest defence of a nation's rights, so a mercenary army is a dreadful danger to a people's liberty, a ready tool in the hand of a tyrant; as heroism with consequent glory is the noble attribute of a patriot, so a mercenary spirit is a stigma on the career of any public officer. We find no fault with an artisan, a merchant, or a common laborer if he estimate the value of his toil by the pecuniary advantages attached to it; for that is the nature of such ordinary occupations, since for man labor is the ordinary and providential condition of existence. But in the higher professions we always look for loftier aspirations. This distinction of rewards for different avocations is so evident that it has passed into the very terms of our language: we speak of "wages" as due to common laborers, of a "salary" as paid to those who render more regular and more intellectual services; of a "fee" as appointed for official and professional actions; and the money paid to a physician or a lawyer is distinguished from ordinary fees by the especial name of "honorary" or "honorarium." This term evidently implies, not only that special honor is due to the recipients of such fees, but besides that the services they render are too noble to be measured in money values, and therefore the money offered is rather in the form of a tribute to a benefactor than of pecuniary compensation for a definite amount of service rendered.

Wages may be measured by the time bestowed, or by the effect produced, or by the wants of the laborer to lead a life of reasonable comfort; a salary is measured by the period of service; but an honorary is not dependent on time employed, or on needs of support, or on effect produced, but it is a tribute of gratitude due to a special benefactor. Whatever practical arrangements may be necessary or excusable in special circumstances, this is the ideal which makes the medical profession so honorable in society.

3. From these and many other considerations that might be added, it is evident, gentlemen, that in the pursuit of the distinguished career for which

you are preparing, you are expected to make yourselves the benefactors of your fellow-men. Now, in order to do so, it will not suffice for you to understand the nature of the various diseases which flesh is heir to, together with the specific powers of every drug described in works on materia medica. The knowledge of anatomy and surgery, and of the various branches that are taught by the many professors with whom I have the honor of being associated in the work of your medical education, no matter how fully that knowledge be mastered, is not sure by itself to make you benefactors to your fellow-men, unless your conduct in the management of all your resources of science and art be directed to procure the real welfare of your patients. Just as a skilful politician may do more harm than good to his country if he direct his efforts to improper ends, or make use of disgraceful means; as a dishonest lawyer may be more potent for the perversion than the maintenance of justice among his fellow-citizens; so likewise an able physician may abuse the beneficent resources of his profession to procure inferior advantages at the sacrifice of moral rights and superior blessings.

Your career, gentlemen, to be truly useful to others and pursued with safety and benefit to yourselves, needs to be directed by a science whose principles it will be my task to explain in this course of lectures—the science of MEDICAL JURISPRUDENCE.

It is the characteristic of science to trace results to their causes. The science of *Jurisprudence* investigates the causes or principles of law. It is defined as "the study of law in connection with its underlying principles." *Medical Jurisprudence*, in its wider sense, comprises two departments, namely, the study of the laws regarding medical practice, and, more, especially, the study of the principles on which those laws are founded, and from which they derive their binding power on the human conscience. The former department, styled *Medical Law*, is assigned in the Prospectus of this College to a gentleman of the legal profession. He will acquaint you with the laws of the land, and of this State in particular, which regulate the practice of medicine; he will explain the points on which a Doctor may come in contact with the law courts, either as a practitioner having to account for his own actions, under a charge of malpractice perhaps, or as an expert summoned as a witness before a court in matters of civil contests or criminal prosecutions. His field is wide and important, but the field of *Medical Jurisprudence,* in its stricter or more specific sense, is wider still and its research much deeper: it considers those principles of reason that underlie the laws of the land, the natural rights and duties which these laws are indeed to enforce to some extent, but which are antecedent and superior to all human laws, being themselves founded on the essential and eternal fitness of things. For things are not right or wrong simply because men have chosen to make them so. You all understand, gentlemen, that, even if we were living in a newly discovered land, where no code of human laws had yet been adopted, nor courts of justice established, nor civil government organized, still even there certain acts of Doctors, as of any other men, would be right and praiseworthy, and others wrong and worthy of condemnation; even there Doctors and patients and their relatives would have certain rights and duties.

In such a land, the lecturer on Medical Law would have nothing to explain; for there would be no human laws and law courts with which a physician could come in contact. But the lecturer on Medical Jurisprudence proper would have as much to explain as I have in this country at present; because he treats of the Ethics or moral principles of Medical Practice, he deals with what is ever the same for all men where-ever they dwell, it being consequent on the very nature of man and his essential relations to his Maker and his fellow-man. Unfortunately the term "Medical Jurisprudence" has been generally misused. Dr. Ewell, in his text-book on the subject, writes "While the term 'Medical Jurisprudence' is a misnomer,—the collection of facts and conclusions usually passing by that name being principally only matters of evidence, and rarely rules of law,—still the term is so generally employed that it would be idle to attempt to bring into use a new term, and we shall accordingly continue the employment of that which has only the sanction of usage to recommend it" (Ch. I).

I prefer to use terms in their genuine meaning; for misnomers are out of place in science, since they are misleading. Yet, to avoid all danger of misunderstanding, I will call my subject "Moral Principles and Medical Practice," and distinctly style it "The Basis of Medical Jurisprudence."

On what lines will my treatment of the subject depart from the beaten path? On the same lines on which most other improvements have been made in the science of medicine. Science has not discovered new laws of physical nature that did not exist before; but it has succeeded in understanding existing laws more perfectly than before, and has shaped its practice accordingly. So, too, the leaders of thought among physicians, especially in English-speaking countries, now understand the laws of moral nature—the principles of Ethics—more thoroughly than most of their predecessors did, and they have modified their treatment so as to conform it to these rules of morality. Hitherto Medical Jurisprudence had regulated the conduct of practitioners by human, positive laws, and sanctioned acts because they were not condemned by civil courts. Now we go deeper in our studies, and appeal from human legislation to the first principles of right and wrong, as Jurisprudence ought to do; and, in consequence, some medical operations which used to be tolerated, or even approved, by many in the profession are at present absolutely and justly condemned. The learned physician these days is no longer afraid to face the moral philosopher; there is no longer any estrangement between Ethics and Medical Practice. Medicine, sent from Heaven to be an angel of mercy to man, is now ever faithful to its beneficent mission; it never more performs the task of a destroying spirit, as—not in wantonness, but in ignorance—it did frequently before.

On these lines, then, of the improved understanding of first principles, I will now proceed to develop the teachings of Medical Jurisprudence.

The first principle that I will lay down for explanation is, that a man is not to be held responsible for all his acts, but only for those which he does of his own free will, which, therefore, it is in his power to do or not to do. These are called *human* acts, because they proceed from a distinctively human power. A brute animal cannot perform such acts; it can only do under given circumstances what its impulses prompt it to do; or, when it experiences various impulses in different directions, it can only follow its strongest impulse; as when a dog, rushing up to attack a man, turns and runs away before his uplifted stick. When a bird sings, it cannot help singing; but a man may sing or not sing at his choice; his singing is a human act. When, however, under the impulse of violent pain, a person happens involuntarily to sigh or groan or even shriek, this indeed is the act of a man, but, inasmuch as it is physically uncontrollable, it is not a human act. So whatever a patient may do while under the influence of chloroform is not a human act, and he is not morally responsible for it. His conduct under the circumstances may denote a brave or a cowardly disposition, or it may indicate habits of self-command or the absence of them. His prayers or curses while thus unconscious are no doubt the effects of acquired virtues or vices; yet, in as far as his will has no share in the present acts, they are not free or human acts. He deserves praise or blame for his former acts, by which he acquired such habits, but not for his unconscious acts as such.

From this principle it follows that a physician is not responsible to God or man for such evil consequences of his prescriptions or surgical operations as are entirely beyond his will and therefore independent of his control. If, however, his mistakes arise from his ignorance or want of skill, he is blamable in as far as he is the wilful cause of such ignorance; he should have known better; or, not knowing better, he should not have undertaken the case for which he knew he was not qualified.

But it often happens that the best informed and most skilful practitioner, even when acting with his utmost care, causes real harm to his patients; he is the accidental, not the wilful, cause of that harm, and therefore he is free from all responsibility in the matter.

The practical lessons, however, which all of you must lay to heart on this subject are: 1st. That you are in duty bound to acquire sound knowledge and great skill in your profession; since the consequences involved are of the greatest moment, your obligation is of a most serious nature. 2d. That in your future practice you will be obliged on all occasions to use all reasonable care for the benefit of your patients. 3d. That you cannot in conscience undertake the management of cases of unusual difficulty unless you possess the special knowledge required, or avail yourselves of the best counsel that can reasonably be obtained.

5. A second principle of Ethics in medical practice, gentlemen, is this, that many human acts may be highly criminal of which, however, human laws and courts take no notice whatsoever. In this matter I am not finding fault with human legislation. The laws of the land, considering the end and the nature of civil government, need take no cognizance of any but overt acts; a man's heart may be a very cesspool of vice, envy, malice, impurity, pride, hatred, etc., yet human law does not and ought not to punish him for this, as long as his actions do not disturb the public peace nor trench upon the happiness of his neighbor. Even his open outward acts which injure only himself, such as gluttony, blasphemy, impiety, private drunkenness, self-abuse, even seduction and fornication, are not usually legislated against or punished in our courts. Does it follow that they are innocent acts and lawful before God? No man in his right senses will say so.

The goodness and the evil of human acts is not dependent on human legislation alone; in many cases the moral good or evil is so intrinsic to the very nature of the acts that God Himself could not change the radical difference between them. Thus justice, obedience to lawful authority, gratitude to benefactors, are essentially good; while injustice, disobedience, and ingratitude are essentially evil. Our reason informs us of this difference; and our reason is nothing else than our very nature as intelligent beings capable of knowing truth. The voice of our reason or conscience is the voice of God Himself, who speaks through the rational nature that He has made. Through our reason God not only tells us of the difference between good and evil acts, but He also commands us to do good and avoid evil;—to do certain acts because they are proper, right, orderly, suitable to the end for which we are created; and to avoid other acts because they are improper, wrong, disorderly, unsuitable to the end of our existence. There is a third class of acts, which, in themselves, are indifferent, i.e., neither good nor evil, neither necessary for our end nor interfering with its attainment. These we are free to do or to omit as we prefer; but even these become good and even obligatory when they are commanded by proper authority, and they become evil when forbidden. In themselves, they are indifferent acts.

6. These explanations are not mere abstractions, gentlemen, or mere philosophical speculations. True, my subject is philosophical; but it is the philosophy of every-day life; we are dealing with live issues which give rise to the gravest discussions of your medical journals; issues on which practically depend the lives of thousands of human beings every year, issues which regard physicians more than any other class of men, and for the proper consideration of which Doctors are responsible to their conscience, to human society, and to their God. To show you how we are dealing with present live issues, let me give you an example of a case in point. In the "Medical Record," an estimable weekly, now in almost the fiftieth year of its existence, there was lately carried on a lengthy and, in some of its parts, a learned discussion, regarding the truth of the principles which I have just now explained, namely, the intrinsic difference between right and wrong, independently of the ruling of law courts and of any human legislation. The subject of the discussion was the lawfulness in any case at all of performing

craniotomy, or of directly destroying the life of the child by any process whatever, at the time of parturition, with the intention of saving the life of the mother.

I will not examine this important matter in all its bearings at present; I mean to take it up later on in our course, and to lay before you the teachings of science on this subject, together with the principles on which they are based. For the present I will confine myself to the point we are treating just now, namely, the existence of a higher law than that of human tribunals, the superiority of the claims of natural to those of legal justice. Some might think, at first sight, that this needs no proof. In fact we are all convinced that human laws are often unjust, or, at least, very imperfect, and therefore they cannot be the ultimate test or fixed standard of right and wrong; yet the main argument advanced by one of the advocates of craniotomy rests upon the denial of a higher law, and the assertion of the authority of human tribunals as final in such matters.

In the "Medical Record" for July 27, 1895, p. 141, this gentleman writes in defence of craniotomy: "The question is a legal one *per se* against which any conflicting view is untenable. The subdivisions under which the common law takes consideration of craniotomy are answers in themselves to the conclusions quoted above, under the unfortunate necessity which demands the operation." Next he quotes the Ohio statute law, which, he remarks, was enacted in protection of physicians who are confronted with this dire necessity. He is answered with much ability and sound learning by Dr. Thomas J. Kearney, of New York, in the same "Medical Record" for August 31, 1895, p. 320, who writes: "Dr. G. bases his argument for the lawfulness of craniotomy in the teachings of common law, contending, at least implicitly, that it is unnecessary to seek farther the desired justification. However, the basis of common law, though broad, is certainly not broad enough for the consideration of such a question as the present one. His coolness rises to sublime heights, in thus assuming infallibility for common law, ignoring the very important fact that behind it there is another and higher law, whose imperative, to every one with a conscience, is ultimate. It evidently never occurs to him that some time could be profitably spent in research, with the view to discovering how often common-law maxims, seen to be at variance with the principles of morality, have been abrogated by statutory enactments. Now the maxims of common law relating to craniotomy, the statutes in conformity therewith, as well as Dr. G.'s arguments (some of them at least), rest on a basis of pure unmitigated expediency; and this is certainly in direct contravention of the teachings of all schools of moral science, even the utilitarian."

Dr. Kearney's doctrine of the existence of a higher law, superior to all human law, is the doctrine that has been universally accepted, in all Christian lands at least, and is so to the present day. Froude explains it correctly when he writes: "Our human laws are but the copies, more or less imperfect, of the eternal laws so far as we can read them, and either succeed and promote our welfare or fail and bring confusion and disaster, according as the legislator's insight has detected the true principle, or has been distorted by ignorance or selfishness" (Century Dict., "Law").

Whoever calmly reflects on the manner in which laws are enacted by legislative bodies, under the influence of human passions and prejudices, often at the dictation of party leaders or of popular sentiment, of office-seekers or wealthy corporations, etc., will not maintain for a moment that human laws and human tribunals are to be accepted as the supreme measure or *norma* of right and wrong. The common law of England, which lies at the basis of our American legislation, and is an integral portion of our civil government, is less fluctuating than our statutory law, and is in the main sound and in conformity with the principles of Jurisprudence. But no one will claim infallibility for its enactments; the esteem we have for it is chiefly due to its general accord with the requirements of the higher law.

7. There is, then, a higher law, which all men are bound to obey, even lawgivers and rulers themselves as well as their humblest subjects, a law from which no man nor class of men can claim exemption, a law which the Creator cannot fail to impose upon His rational creatures: although God was free to create or not to create as He chose, since He did not need anything to complete His own happiness,—yet, if He did create, He was bound by His own wisdom to put order into His work; else it would not be worthy of His supreme wisdom. As the poet has so tersely expressed it, "Order is Heaven's first law."

How admirably is this order displayed in the material universe! The more we study the sciences—astronomy, biology, botany, physiology, medicine, etc.—the more we are lost in admiration at the beautiful order we see displayed in the tiniest as well as in the vastest portions of the creation. And shall man alone, the masterpiece of God in this visible universe, be allowed to be disorderly, to be a failure in the noblest part of his being, to make himself like to the brute or to a demon of malice, to waste his choicest gifts in the indulgence of debasing pleasure? The Creator is bound by His own wisdom to direct men to high purposes, worthy of their exalted intellectual nature. But how shall He direct man? He compels material things to move with order to the accomplishment of their alloted tasks by the physical laws of matter. He directs brute animals most admirably to run their appointed careers by the wonderful laws of instinct, which none of them can resist at will. But man He has made free; He must direct him to do worthy actions by means suitable to a free being, that is, by the enacting of the moral law.

He makes known to us what is right and wrong. He informs every one of us, by the voice of reason itself, that He requires us to do the right and avoid the wrong. He has implanted in us the sense of duty to obey that law. If we do so, we lead worthy lives, we please Him, and, in His goodness, He has rewards in store.

But can He be pleased with us if we thwart His designs; if we, His noblest works on earth, instead of adding to the universal harmony of His creation, make monsters of ourselves, moral blots upon the beautiful face of His world? It were idle for Him to give us the knowledge of His will and then to stand by and let us disfigure His fairest designs; to bid us do what is right, and then let us do wrong without exacting redress or atonement. If He is wise, He must not only lay down the law, but He must also enforce it; He must make it our highest interest to keep His law, to do the right; so that ultimately those men shall be happy who have done it, and those who have thwarted His designs shall be compelled to rue it. He will not deprive us of liberty, the fairest gift to an intelligent creature, but He will hold out rewards and punishments to induce us to keep the law and to avoid its violation. Once He has promised and threatened, His justice and His holiness compel Him to fulfil His threats and promises. A man can commit no rasher act than to ignore, defy, and violate that higher law of which we are speaking, and which, if it must direct all men, especially requires the respect and obedience of those into whose hands he has placed at times the lives of their fellow-men, the greatest of earthly treasures.

I have insisted so much, gentlemen, on the existence of the higher law, on its binding power and on the necessity of observing it, because it is the foundation of my whole course of lectures. If there were no higher law, then there would be no Medical Jurisprudence, in the true sense of the word. For Jurisprudence studies the principles that underlie legal enactments, and if there were no higher law, there would be no such principles; then the knowledge of the human law would fill the whole programme. This in fact is the contention of the defendant of craniotomy to whom I have referred; and he boldly applies his speculation to a matter in which the physician has the most frequent opportunity to exhibit his fidelity to principle, or his subserviency to the requirements of temporary expediency at the sacrifice of duty.

8. You will find, gentlemen, as we proceed in our course, that Doctors have very many occasions in which to apply the lessons of Jurisprudence in their medical practice. I even suspect that they need to be more conscientious in regard to the dictates of the higher law than any other class of men, the clergy alone, perhaps, excepted. They need this not only for their own good, but also for the good of their patients and of the community at large. The reasons are these:

A. The matters entrusted to their keeping are the most important of all earthly possessions; for they are life itself, and, along with life, health, the necessary condition of almost all temporal enjoyment. No other class of men is entrusted with more weighty earthly interests. Hence the physician's responsibility is very great; hence the common good requires that he be eminently faithful and conscientious.

B. With no other class of men does the performance of duty depend more on personal integrity, on conscientious regard for the higher law of morality than with the Doctor. For the Doctor's conduct is less open to observation than that of other professions. The lawyer may have many temptations to act unjustly; but other lawyers are watching him, and the courts of justice are at hand to check his evil practices. As to the judge, he is to pronounce his decisions in public and give reasons for his ruling. The politician is jealously watched by his political opponents. The public functionary, if he is unjust in his dealings, is likely sooner or later to be brought to an account. But the physician, on very many occasions, can be morally sure that his conduct will never be publicly scrutinized. Such is the nature of his ministrations, and such too is the confidence habitually reposed in his integrity, that he is and must be implicitly trusted in matters in which, if he happens to be unworthy of his vocation, he may be guilty of the most outrageous wrongs.

The highest interests of earth are in his hands. If he is not conscientious, or if he lets himself be carried about by every wind of modern speculations, he can readily persuade himself that a measure is lawful because it is presently expedient, that acts can justly be performed because the courts do not punish them; and thus he will often violate the most sacred rights of his patients or of their relatives. Who has more frequent opportunities than a licentious Doctor to seduce the innocent, to pander to the passions of the guilty, to play into the hands of greedy heirs, who may be most willing to pay him for his services? No one can do it more safely, as far as human tribunals are concerned. As a matter of fact, many, all over this land and other lands, are often guilty of prostituting their noble profession to the vilest uses. The evil becomes all the more serious when false doctrines are insinuated, or publicly advocated, which throw doubt upon the most sacred principles of morality. True, the sounder and by far the larger portion of medical men protest against these false teachings by their own conduct at least; but it very frequently happens that the honest man is less zealous in his advocacy of what is right than is the propagandist of bold speculations and dangerous new theories in the spreading of what is pernicious.

The effect thus produced upon many minds is to shake their convictions, to say the least; and I need not tell you, gentlemen, that weak convictions are not likely to be proof against violent and repeated temptations. In fact, if a physician, misled by any of those many theories which are often inculcated or at least insinuated by false scientists, can ever convince himself, or even can begin to surmise that, after all, there may be no such thing as a higher law before which he is responsible for even his secret conduct, then what is to prevent him from becoming a dangerous person to the community? If he see much temporal gain on the one hand, and security from legal prosecution on the other, what would keep him in the path of duty and honesty? Especially if he can once make himself believe that, for all he knows, he may be nothing more than a rather curiously developed lump of matter, which is to lose forever all consciousness in death. Why should he not get rid of any other evolved lump of matter if it stand in the way of his present or prospective happiness? Those are dangerous men who inculcate such theories; it were a sad day for the medical profession and for the world at large if ever they found much countenance among physicians. Society cannot do without the higher law; this law is to be studied in Medical Jurisprudence.

It is my direct object, gentlemen, to explain this law to you in its most important bearings, and thus to lay before you the chief duties of your profession. The principal reason why I have undertaken to deliver this course of lectures—the chief reason, in fact, why the Creighton University has assumed the management of this Medical College—is that we wish to provide for the West, as far as we are able, a goodly supply of conscientious physicians, who shall be as faithful and reliable as they will be able and well informed; whose solid principles and sterling integrity shall be guarantees of upright and virtuous conduct.

That this task of mine may be successfully accomplished, I will endeavor to answer all difficulties and objections that you may propose. I will never consider it a want of respect to me as your professor if you will urge your questions till I have answered them to your full satisfaction. On the contrary, I request you to be very inquisitive; and I will be best pleased with those who show themselves the most ready to point out those difficulties, connected with my lectures, which seem to require further answers and explanations.

LECTURE II.
CRANIOTOMY.

Gentlemen:—In my first lecture I proved to you the existence and the binding power of a higher law than that of human legislators, namely, of the eternal law, which, in His wisdom, the Creator, if He created at all, could not help enacting, and which He is bound by His wisdom and justice to enforce upon mankind.

We are next to consider what are the duties which that higher law imposes upon the physician. In this present lecture I will confine myself to one duty, that of respect for human life.

A duty is a bond imposed on our will. God, as I remarked before, imposes such bonds, and by them He directs free beings to lead worthy lives. As He directs matter by irresistible physical laws, so He directs intelligent and free beings by moral laws, that is, by laying duties or moral bonds upon them, which they ought to obey, which He must require them to obey, enforcing His commands by suitable rewards and punishments. Thus He establishes and enforces the moral order.

Now the duties He lays upon us are of three classes. First, there are duties of reverence and honor towards Himself as our sovereign Lord and Master. These are called the duties of Religion, the study of which does not belong to Medical Jurisprudence. The other classes of duties regard ourselves and our fellow-men, with these we are to deal in our lectures.

I. Order requires that the meaner species of creatures shall exist for the benefit of the nobler; the inert clod of earth supports vegetable life, the vegetable kingdom supplies the wants of animal life, the brute animal with all inferior things subserves the good of man; while man, the master of the visible universe, himself exists directly for the honor and glory of God. In this beautiful order of creation, man can use all inferior things for his own benefit.

This is what reason teaches concerning our status in this world; and this teaching of reason is confirmed by the convictions of all nations and all ages of mankind. The oldest page of literature that has come down to us, namely, the first chapter of the first book of Holy Writ, lays down this same law, and no improvement has been made in it during all subsequent ages. Whether we regard this writing as inspired, as Christians and Jews have always done, or only as the testimony of the most remote antiquity, confirmed by the acceptance of all subsequent generations, it is for every sensible man of the highest authority.

Here is the passage: "God said, Let us make man to our image and likeness; and let him have dominion over the fishes of the sea, and the fowls of the air, and the beasts, and the whole earth, and every creeping creature that creepeth upon the earth." And later on in history, after the deluge, God more explicitly declared the order thus established, saying to Noe and his posterity: "Every thing that moveth and liveth shall be meat for you; even as the green herbs have I delivered them to you." But He emphatically adds that the lives of men are not included in this grant; they are directly reserved for His own disposal. "At the hand of every man," He says, "will I require the life of man."

All things then are created for man; man is created directly for God, and is not to be sacrificed for the advantage of a fellow-man. Thus reason and Revelation in unison proclaim that we can use brute animals as well as plants for our benefit, taking away their lives when it is necessary or useful to do so for our own welfare; while no man is ever allowed to slay his fellow-man for his own use or benefit: "At the hand of every man will I require the life of man."

II. The first practical application I will make of these general principles to the conduct of physicians is this: a physician and a student of medicine can, with a safe conscience, use any brute animal that has not been appropriated by another man, whether it be bug or bird or beast, to experiment upon, whatever specious arguments humane societies may advance to the contrary. Brute animals are for the use of man, for his food and clothing, his mental and physical improvement, and even his reasonable recreations. Man can lawfully hunt and fish and practise his skill at the expense of the brute creation, notwithstanding the modern fad of sentimentalists. The teacher and the pupil can use vivisection, and thus to some extent prolong the sufferings of the brute subject for the sake of science, of mental improvement, and intelligent observation. But is not this cruelty? and has a man a right to be cruel? No man has a right to be cruel; cruelty is a vice, it is degrading to man's noble nature. But vivisection practised for scientific purposes is not cruel. Cruelty implies the *wanton* infliction of pain: there are people who delight in seeing a victim tortured; this is cruelty or savagery, and is a disgrace to man. Even to inflict pain without benefit is cruel and wrong; but not when it is inflicted on the brute creation for the benefit of man, unless the pain should be very great and the benefit very small. Certainly it is right to cultivate habits of kindness even to animals; but this matter must not be carried to excess.

The teaching of humane societies condemning all vivisection is due to the exaggeration of a good sentiment and to ignorance of first principles. For they suppose that sufferings inflicted on brute animals are a violation of their rights. Now we maintain that brute animals have no rights in the true sense of the word. To prove this thesis we must explain what a right is and how men get to have rights. A *right* is a moral claim to a thing, which claim other persons are obliged to respect. Since every man has a destiny appointed for him by his Creator, and which he is to work out by his own acts, he must have the means given him to do so. For to assign a person a task and not to give him the means of accomplishing it would be absurd. Therefore the Creator wants him to have those means, and forbids every one to deprive him of those means. Here is the foundation of rights. Every man, in virtue of the Creator's will, has certain advantages or claims to advantages assigned him which no other man may infringe. Those advantages and claims constitute his rights, guaranteed him by the Creator; and all other men have the *duty* imposed on them to respect those rights. Thus rights and duties are seen to be correlative and inseparable; the rights lodged in one man beget duties in other men. The same Creator that assigns rights to one man lays upon all others duties to respect those rights, that thus every free being may have the means of working out its Heaven-appointed destiny.

Thus it is apparent that rights and duties suppose free beings, persons; now an irrational animal is not a person; it is not a free being, having a destiny to work out by its free acts; it is therefore incapable of having duties. Duties are matters of conscience; therefore they cannot belong to the brute animal; for it has no conscience. And, since rights are given to creatures because of the duties incumbent on them, brute animals are incapable of having rights. When a brute animal has served man's purpose, it has reached its destiny.

III. But it is entirely different with man: there is what we may call an infinite distance between man and brute. Every man is created directly for the honor and service not of other men, but of God Himself: by serving God man must work out his own destiny—eternal happiness. In this respect all men are equal, having the same essence or nature and the same destiny. The poor child has as much right to attain eternal happiness as the rich child, the infant as much as the gray-bearded sire. Every one is only at the beginning of an endless existence, of which he is to determine the nature by his own free acts. In this infinite destiny lies the infinite superiority of man over the brute creation.

That all men are equal in their essential rights is the dictate of common-sense and of sound philosophy. This truth may not flatter kings and princes; but it is the charter of human rights, founded deeper and broader in nature and on the Creator's will than any other claim of mankind. As order requires the subordination of lower natures to higher, so it requires equality of essential rights among beings of the same nature. Now all men are of the same nature, hence they have all the same essential rights.

If any people on earth must stand by these principles, certainly the American people must do so; for we have put them as the foundation-stones of our civil liberty. There is more wisdom than many, even of its admirers, imagine in the preamble to our Declaration of Independence; upon it we are to base the most important rights and duties which belong to Jurisprudence. The words of the preamble read as follows: "We hold these truths as self-evident, that all men are created equal; that they are endowed by their Creator with certain inalienable rights; that among these are life, liberty, and the pursuit of happiness." I feel convinced, gentlemen, and I will take it for granted henceforth, unless you bring objections to the contrary, that you all agree with me on this important point that *every man has a natural right to his life, a right which all other men are solemnly bound to respect.* It is his chief earthly right. It is called an *inalienable* right; by which term the fathers of our liberty meant a right which under no circumstances can be lawfully disregarded. A man who takes it upon himself to deprive another of life commits two grievous wrongs: one towards his victim, whose most important right he violates, and one towards God, who has a right to the life and service of His creatures. "Thou shalt not kill" is a precept as deeply engraven on the human heart by reason itself as it was on the stone tables of the Ten Commandments by Revelation.

So far we have chiefly considered murder as a violation of man's right to his life. We must now turn our attention to God's right, which the murderer violates. It may indeed happen that a man willingly resigns his right to live, that he is tired of life, and longs and implores for some one to take it away. Can you then do it? You cannot. His life does not belong to him alone, but to God also, and to God principally; if you destroy it, you violate God's right, and you will have to settle with Him. God wills this man to live and serve Him, if it were only by patient endurance of his sufferings.

For a man may be much ennobled and perfected by the practice of patience under pain and agony. Some of the noblest characters of history are most glorious for such endurance. The suicide rejects this greatness; he robs God of service and glory, he rebels against his Creator. Even Plato of old understood the baseness of suicide, when he wrote in his dialogue called "Phædon" that a man in this world is like a soldier stationed on guard; he must hold his post as long as his commander requires it; to desert it is cowardice and treachery; thus, he says, suicide is a grievous crime.

This being so, can a Doctor, or any other man, ever presume to contribute his share to the shortening of a person's life by aiding him to commit suicide? We must emphatically say No, even though the patient should desire death: the Doctor cannot, in any case, lend his assistance to violate the right and the law of the Creator: "Thou shalt not kill."

I have no doubt, gentlemen, that some of you have been saying to yourselves, Why does the lecturer insist so long upon a point which is so clear? Of course, none of us doubts that we can in no case aid a patient to commit suicide. My reason for thus insisting on this matter is that here again we are dealing with a living issue. There are to-day physicians and others who deny this truth, not in their secret practice only, but, of late, to justify their conduct, they have boldly formulated the thesis that present apparent expediency can lawfully be preferred to any higher consideration. Here is the fact. At a Medico-Legal Congress, held in the summer of 1895, Dr. Bach, one of its leading lights, openly maintained it as his opinion that

"Physicians have the moral right to end life when the disease is incurable, painful, and agonizing."

What his arguments were in support of his startling proposition, I have not been able to learn. But I know that a cry of horror and indignation has gone up from many a heart. Many have protested in print; but unless, on an occasion like this, moralists raise their voice against it with all the influence which sound principles command, the saying of Dr. Bach may at least shake the convictions of the rising generation of physicians. The only argument for Dr. Bach's assertion that I can imagine—and it is one proceeding from the heart rather than the head—is that it is cruel to let a poor man suffer when there is no longer hope of recovery. It is not the Physician that makes him suffer; it is God who controls the case, and God is never cruel.

He knows His own business, and forbids you to thwart His designs. If the sufferer be virtuous, God has an eternity to reward his patient endurance; if guilty, the Lord often punishes in this world that He may spare in the next. Let Him have His way, if you are wise; His command to all is clear, "Thou shalt not kill."

One rash utterance, like that of Dr. Bach, can do an incalculable amount of harm. Why, gentlemen, just think what consequences must follow if his principle were, admitted! For the only reason that could give it any plausibility would be that the patient's life is become useless and insupportable. If that were a reason for taking human life away, then it would follow that, whenever a man considers his life as useless and no longer supportable, he could end it, he could commit suicide. That reasoning would practically justify almost all suicides. For, when people kill themselves, it is, in almost all cases, because they consider their lives useless and insupportable. Whether it results from physical or from moral causes that they consider their life a burden, cannot, it seems to me, make any material difference; grief, shame, despair are as terrible sufferings as bodily pains. If, then, we accept Dr. Bach's principle, we must be prepared for all its baneful consequences.

IV. But are there no exceptions to the general law, "Thou shalt not kill"? Are there no cases in which it is allowed to take another's life? What about justifiable homicide? There are three cases of this nature, gentlemen; namely, self-defence, capital punishment inflicted by the state, and active warfare. With only one of these can a physician, as such be concerned or think himself concerned. He is not a public hangman executing a sentence of a criminal court; nor is he acting as a soldier proceeding by public authority against a public foe. As to the plea of self-defence, it must be correctly understood, lest he usurp a power which neither human nor divine law has conferred upon him.

1. *Self-defence.* It is a dictate of common-sense, already quoted by Cicero as a universally received maxim of Jurisprudence in his day, that it is justifiable to repel violence by violence, even if the death of our unjust assailant should result. In such a case, let us consider what really takes place. A ruffian attempts to take away my life; I have a right to my life. I may, therefore, protect it against him; and, for that purpose, I may use all lawful means. A lawful means is one that violates no law, one that I may use without giving any one reasonable ground of complaint. Suppose I have no other means to protect my life than by shooting my aggressor; has he a right to complain of my conduct if I try to do so? No, because he forces me to the act; he forces me to choose between my life and his. Good order is not violated if I prefer my own life: well-ordered charity begins at home. But is not God's right violated? It is; for God has a right to my life and to that of my assailant. The ruffian who compels me to shoot him is to blame for bringing both our lives into danger; he is responsible for it to God. But the Creator will not blame me for defending my life by the only means in my power, and that when compelled by an unjust assailant, who cannot reasonably find fault with my conduct.

But it may be objected that no evil act may be done to procure a good result, that a good end does not justify a bad means. That is a correct principle, and we will consider it carefully some other day. But my act of necessary self-defence is not evil, and therefore needs no justification; for the means I employ are, under the circumstances, well-ordered and lawful means, which violate no one's rights, as has just been shown. Of course the harm I do to the aggressor is just only in as far as it is strictly necessary to defend the inalienable right I have to life or limb or very valuable property. Hence I must keep within the just limits of self-defence. To shoot an assailant, when I am in no serious danger, or when I can free myself some other way, or when I act through malice, would not be self-defence, but unjustifiable violence on my part.

2. The principles that make it lawful for a man to defend his own life with violence against an unjust assailant will also justify a parent in thus defending his children, a guardian his wards; and in fact any one may forcibly defend any other human being against unjust violence. A parent or guardian not only can, but he is in duty bound to, defend those under his charge by all lawful means. Similarly the physician would be obliged to defend his patient by the exercise of his profession in his behalf.

Now the only case in which the need of medical treatment against unjust aggression could become a matter for discussion in Jurisprudence is the case of a mother with child. Is the child under those circumstances really an unjust aggressor? Let us study that important case with the closest attention. Let all the rays of light we have gathered so far be focussed on this particular point. Can a physician ever be justified in destroying the life of a child, before or during its birth, by craniotomy or in any other manner, in order to save its mother's life, on the plea that the child is an unjust assailant of the life of its mother? Put the case in a definite shape before you. Here is a mother in the pangs of parturition. An organic defect, no matter in what shape or form, prevents deliverance by the ordinary channels. All that medical skill can do to assist nature has been done. The case is desperate. Other physicians have been called in for consultation, as the civil law requires before it will tolerate extreme measures. All agree that, if no surgical operation is performed, both mother and child must die. There are the Cæsarian section, the Porro operation, laparotomy, symphysiotomy, all approved by science and the moral law. But we will suppose an extreme case; namely, the circumstances are so unfavorable for any of these operations—whether owing to want of skill in the Doctors present, or for any other reason—that none can safely be attempted; any of them would be fatal to the mother.

In this extreme case of necessity, can the Doctor break the cranium of the living child, or in any way destroy its life with a view to save the mother? If three consulting physicians agree that this is the only way to save her, he will not be molested by the law courts for performing the murderous operation. But will the law of nature and of nature's God approve or allow his conduct? This is the precise question under our consideration. We have seen that the infant, a true human being, has a right to live, as well as its mother. "All men are created equal, and have an equal right to life," declares the first principle of our liberty. The Creator, too, as reason teaches, has a clear right to the child's life; that child may answer a very special purpose of Providence. But whether it will or not, God is the supreme and the only Master of life and death, and He has laid down the strict prohibition, "Thou shalt not kill."

Now comes the plea of self-defence against an unjust aggressor. If the child is such, if it *unjustly* attacks its mother's life, then she can destroy it to save herself, and her physician can aid the innocent against the guilty party. But can it be proved that the infant is an unjust aggressor in the case? There can be no intentional or *formal* guilt in the little innocent babe. But can we argue that the actual situation of the child is an unjust act, unconsciously done, yet *materially* unjust, unlawful? Thus, if a madman would rush at me with a sharp sword, evidently intent on killing me, he may be called an unjust aggressor; though, being a raving maniac, he does not know what crime he is committing, and is *formally* innocent of murderous intent. *Materially* considered, the act is unjust, and I can defend myself lawfully as against any other unjust assailant. Such is the common teaching of moralists. But can the innocent babe be classed in the same category with the raving maniac? Why should it? It is doing nothing; it is merely passive in the whole process of parturition.

Will any one object that the infant has no right to be there at all? Who put it there? The only human agents in the matter were its parents. The mother is more accountable for the unfortunate situation than the child. Certainly you could not, to save the child, directly kill the mother, treating her as an unjust assailant of her child's life? Still less can you treat the infant as an unjust assailant of its mother's life.

The plea of self-defence against unjust aggression being thus ruled out of court in all such cases, and no other plea remaining for the craniotomist, we have established, on the clearest principles of Ethics and Jurisprudence, that it is never allowed directly to kill a child as a means to save its mother's life. It would be a bad means, morally evil; and no moral evil can ever be done that good may come of it; the end cannot justify an evil means. In theory all good men agree with us that the end can never justify the means. But in practice it seems to be different with some of the medical profession. Of late, however, the practice of craniotomy and all equivalent operations upon living subjects has gone almost entirely out of fashion among the better class of physicians.

Allow me, gentlemen, to conclude this lecture with the reading of two extracts from articles of medical writers on the present state of craniotomy in their profession. You will find them in accord with the conclusions at which we have arrived by reasoning upon the principles of Jurisprudence.

Dr. W. H. Parish writes ("Am. Eccles. Review," November, 1893, p. 364): "The operations of craniotomy and embryotomy are to-day of relatively infrequent occurrence, and many obstetricians of large experience have never performed them. Advanced obstetricians advocate the performance of the Cesarian section or its modification—the Porro operation—in preference to craniotomy, because nearly all the children are saved, and the unavoidable mortality among mothers is not much higher than that which attends craniotomy. Of one hundred women on whom Cesarian section is performed under *favorable conditions* and with *attainable* skill, about ninety-five mothers should recover and fully the same number of children. Of one hundred craniotomies, ninety-five mothers or possibly a larger number will recover, and of course none of the children. The problem resolves itself into this: Which shall we choose—Cesarian section with one hundred and ninety living beings as the result, or craniotomy with about ninety-five living beings?"

Even if a liberal deduction be made for unfavorable circumstances and deficient skill, the results, gentlemen, will still leave a wide margin in favor of Cesarian section. My second extract is from an article of Dr. M. O'Hara, and it is supported by the very highest authorities (ib. p. 361): "Recently [August 1, 1893] the British Medical Association, the most authoritative medical body in Great Britain, at its sixty-first annual meeting, held at Newcastle-upon-Tyne, definitely discussed the subject before us. In the address delivered at the opening of the section of Obstetric Medicine and Gynecology, an assertion was put forth which I regard as very remarkable, my recollection not taking in any similar pronouncement made in any like representative medical body. The authoritative value of this statement, accepted as undisputed by the members of the association, which counts about fifteen thousand practitioners, need not be emphasized.

"Dr. James Murphy ('British Medical Journal,' August 26, 1893), of the University of Durham, made the presidential address. He first alluded to the perfection to which the forceps had reached for pelves narrowed at the brim, and the means of correcting faulty position of the fœtus during labor. He then stated: 'In cases of great deformity of the pelvis, it has long been the ambition of the obstetrician, where it has been impossible to deliver a living child *per vias naturales,* to find some means by which that child could be born alive with comparative safety to the mother; and that time has now arrived. It is not for me to decide,' he says, 'whether the modern Cesarian section, Porro's operation, symphysiotomy, ischiopubotomy, or other operation is the safest or most suitable, nor yet is there sufficient material for this question to be decided; but when such splendid and successful results have been achieved by Porro, Leopold, Saenger, and by our own Murdoch Cameron, I say it deliberately and with whatever authority I possess, and I urge it with all the force I can master, that we are not now justified in destroying a living child; and while there may be some things I look back upon with pleasure in my professional career, that which gives me the greatest satisfaction is that I have never done a craniotomy on a living child.'"

You will please notice, gentlemen, that when this distinguished Doctor said, "We are not *now* justified in destroying a living child," he was speaking from a medical standpoint, and meant to say that such destruction is now scientifically unjustifiable, is a blunder in surgery. From a moral point of view it is not only now, but it was always, unjustifiable to slay a child as a means to save the mother's life; a good end cannot justify an evil means, is a truth that cannot be too emphatically inculcated. This is one of the most important subjects on which Medical Jurisprudence has been improved, and most of its text-books are deficient. The improvement is explained with much scientific detail in an address of the President, Samuel C. Busey, M.D., before the Washington Obstetrical and Gynecological Society ("Am. Journal of Obstetrics and Diseases of Women and Children," vol. xvii. n. 2).

LECTURE III.
ABORTION.

Abortion, gentlemen, is the theme of my present lecture.

I. An important point to be determined is the precise time when the human embryo is first animated by its own specific principle of life, its human soul. It is interesting to read what various conjectures have been ventured on this subject by the learned of former ages. They were totally at sea. Though gifted with keen minds, they had not the proper data to reason from. And yet some of those sages made very shrewd guesses. For instance, as early as the fourth century of our era, St. Gregory of Nyssa taught the true doctrine, which modern science has now universally accepted. He taught that the rational soul is created by Almighty God and infused into the embryo at the very moment of conception. Still, as St. Gregory could not prove the certainty of his doctrine, it was opposed by the majority of the learned.

The Schoolmen of the Middle Ages, while condemning abortion from the time of conception, preferred the opinion of Aristotle, that the rational soul is not infused till the fœtus is sufficiently developed to receive it. The embryo lived first, they taught, with a vegetable life; after a few days an animal soul replaced the vegetative principle; the human soul was not infused into the tiny body till the fortieth day for a male, and the eightieth day for a female child. All this sounds very foolish now; and yet we should not sneer at their ignorance; had we lived in their times, we could probably have done no better than they.

It was not till 1620 that Fienus, a physician of Louvain, in Belgium, published the first book of modern times that came near the truth. He maintained that the human soul was created and infused into the embryo three days after conception. Nearly forty years later, in 1658, a religious priest, called Florentinius, wrote a book in which he taught that, for all we know, the soul may be intellectual or human from the first moment of conception; and the Pope's physician Zachias soon after maintained the thesis as a certainty that the human embryo has from the very beginning a human soul.

Great writers applauded Fienus and his successors; universities favored their views; the Benedictines, the Dominicans, and the Jesuits supported them. Modern science claims to have proved beyond all doubt that the same soul animates the man that animated the fœtus from the very moment of conception. The "Medical Jurisprudence" of Wharton and Stillé quotes Dr. Hodge of the Pennsylvania University as follows (p. 11): "In a most mysterious manner brought into existence, how wonderful its formation! Imperfect in the first instance, nay, even invisible to the naked eye, the embryo is nevertheless endowed, at once, with the principles of vitality; and although retained in the system of its mother, it has, in a strict sense, an independent existence. It immediately manifests all the phenomena of *organic* life; it forms its own fluids and circulates them; it is nourished and developed; and, very rapidly from being a *rudis indigestaque moles*, apparently an inorganic drop of fluid, its organs are generated and its form perfected. It daily gains strength and grows; and, while still within the organ of its mother, manifests some of the phenomena of animal life, especially as regards mobility. After the fourth month its motions are perceptible to the mother, and in a short period can be perceived by other individuals on close investigation.

"The usual impression," the authors add, "and one which is probably still maintained by the mass of the community, is that the embryo is perfected at the period of quickening—say the one hundred and twelfth or one hundred and twentieth day. When the mother first perceives motion, is considered the period when the fœtus becomes animated—when it receives its spiritual nature into union with its corporeal.

"These and similar suppositions are, as has been already shown, contrary to all fact, and, if it were not for the high authorities—medical, legal, and theological—in opposition, we might add, to common-sense."

At present, gentlemen, there seems to be no longer any authority to the contrary. But many people, and some Doctors, seem to be several generations behind the times; for they still act and reason as if in the first weeks of pregnancy no immortal or human soul were in question.

Physicians worthy of their noble profession should strive to remove such gross and mischievous ignorance. In many of the United States the law casts its protection around an unborn infant from its first stage of ascertainable existence; no matter whether "quickening" has taken place or not, and consequently no matter what may be the stage of gestation, an indictment lies for its wilful destruction (Wharton and Stillé, p. 861). "Where there has been as yet no judicial settlement of the immediate question, it may be reasonably contended that to make the criminality of the offence depend upon the fact of quickening is as repugnant to sound morals as it is to enlightened physiology" (ib.). "That it is inconsistent with the analogies of the law is shown by the fact that an infant, born even at the extreme limit of gestation after its father's death, is capable of taking by descent, and being appointed executor" (ib.). Dr. Hodge adds this sensible remark: "It is *then* only [at conception] the father can in any way exert an influence over his offspring; it is *then* only the female germ is in direct union with the mother—the connection afterwards is indirect and imperfect" (ib.). The fact, therefore, is now scientifically established that the embryo from the first moment of conception or fecundation is a human being, having a human immortal soul.

II. Now we come to the direct study of abortion. Abortion, or miscarriage, strictly means the expulsion of the fœtus before it is viable, i.e., before it is sufficiently developed to continue its life outside of the maternal womb. The period of arrival at viability is usually after the twenty-eighth week of gestation. When birth occurs later than that period, and yet before the full term of nine months, it is called *premature birth*, which is altogether different from abortion; for it may save the life of the child, which abortion always destroys. "Premature labor is frequently induced in legitimate medical practice, for the purpose of avoiding the risks which in some cases attend parturition at term.... The average number of children saved by this means is rather more than one-half of the cases operated upon," say Wharton and Stillé ("Parturition," p. 96). But they caution the physician against too ready recourse to this treatment; for, they add very truly, "The sympathetic phenomena of pregnancy are often more alarming in appearance than in reality, and will rarely justify any interference with the natural progress of gestation. In all cases the physician should consult with one or more of his colleagues before inducing premature labor; in this manner his humane intentions will not expose him, in case of failure, to reproach, suspicion, or prosecution."

The first time my attention was practically called to the case of a child in danger of dying before the time of delivery occurred over twenty years ago, when the mother of a highly respected family, then in my spiritual charge, was wasting away with consumption during her state of pregnancy. You know that we Catholics are very solicitous that infants shall not die without Baptism, because we believe that heaven is not promised to the unbaptized. I therefore directed the lady's husband to consult their family physician on the prospects of the case, and take timely precautions, so that, if death should come on the mother before her delivery, the infant might be reached at once and be baptized before it expired. The physician, a learned and conscientious practitioner, answered that we should not be solicitous;

for that Nature had so provided that mothers in such cases rarely die before the child is born. He was right. The child was born and baptized; the mother died a few hours later; the little one lived several weeks before it went to join the angels in heaven. I learned from that occurrence the lesson which Wharton and Stillé inculcate that "the phenomena of pregnancy are often far more alarming in appearance than in reality, and we are rarely justified in interfering with the natural progress of gestation."

To return to our subject. Abortion, or miscarriage, is often, as you know, gentlemen, the result of natural causes beyond human control; at other times it is brought on by unintentional imprudence on the part of the mother or her attendants. It is the duty of the family physician, when occasions offer, to instruct his pregnant patients and other persons concerned on the dangers to be avoided. A good Doctor should be to his patients what a father is to his children; very important matters are confided to him, and therefore grave responsibilities rest on his conscience.

III. We are now ready to consider the chief question of this lecture, namely, whether there can be any cases in which a physician is justified in bringing about an abortion, or in prescribing a treatment from which he knows an abortion is likely to result.

1. It is evident that, if he acts with due prudence, and yet, from some cause which he did not foresee and could not have been foreseen, his treatment brings about a miscarriage, he cannot justly be held accountable for what he could not help.

2. But what if he foresees that a drug or treatment, which, he thinks, is needed for the mother's health, may perhaps bring on a miscarriage? Can he still administer that drug or prescribe that treatment? Notice the question carefully. It is not supposed that he wants to bring on the miscarriage. He does not; he will do all he can to prevent it. Nor will his treatment or drug directly destroy the life or the organism of the embryo; but it is intended to affect favorably the system of the mother, and it is applied to her own

organism. Still the Doctor knows that the prescription may indirectly bring about abortion. Can he prescribe the drug or treatment from which he knows the death of the fœtus may indirectly result, the direct purpose being to remove an ailment of the mother's?

There is a sound moral principle bearing on such cases; it is universally admitted in Ethics and Jurisprudence, and its application is so extensive that it well deserves careful study. It is this: "He who wilfully puts a cause is answerable for the effect of that cause," *causa causæ est causa causati*. Therefore, if the effect is evil, he is answerable for that evil. This, however, supposes that he could foresee the danger of such evil effect.

That evil effect is said to be *indirectly* willed; for it follows from a cause which is *directly* willed. If, then, you should give a dose to a pregnant mother which is intended to stop her fever or other ailment, but may also bring on abortion, the stopping of her fever is directly intended, and the abortion is said to be indirectly intended or willed. Those are the received terms in moral science. It were more correct to say that the abortion in this case is an effect not intended at all, but only *permitted*. That, then, which is permitted to result from our acts is said to be indirectly willed.

Are we then always responsible for evil effects permitted or indirectly willed? The principle laid down seems to say so. But then that principle admits of important exceptions. If we could never do an act from which we know evil consequences may follow, then we could scarcely do anything of importance; a young man could certainly not become a physician at all, for he is almost certain to injure some of his patients in the course of his professional life. But if we had no Doctors, such a loss would be a much greater evil to mankind than their occasional mistakes. Here then we seem to be in a dilemma, with evil on both sides of us. And then we are reminded of that other principle of which we spoke before, that we may never do evil at all that good may come of it. What shall we do? The solution is this: we should never *do* evil, but we are often justified in *permitting* evil to happen;

in other words, we can never will evil *directly*, but we can often will it *indirectly*: we can do what is right in itself, even though we know or fear that evil will also result from our good act.

This conduct requires four conditions: 1. That we do not wish the evil itself, but make all reasonable effort to avoid it. 2. That the immediate effect we wish to produce is good in itself. 3. That the good effect intended is at least as important as the evil effect permitted. 4. That the evil is not made a means used to obtain the good effect.

Now let us apply these principles to the case in hand.

1. If the medicine is necessary to save the mother's life, and it is not certain to bring on abortion, though it is likely to do so, then the good effect is greater and more immediate or direct than the bad effect; then give the medicine to save the mother, and permit the probable death of the child.

2. If the medicine is not necessary to save the mother's life, though very useful, for the sake of such an advantage, you cannot justly expose the child's life to serious danger.

3. But if the danger it is exposed to is not serious but slight, and the remedy, though not necessary, is expected to be very useful to the mother, you may then administer the medicine; for a slight risk need not prevent a prudent man from striving to obtain very good results.

4. But what if the drug is necessary to save the mother, and as dangerous to the child as it is beneficial to her; can you then give the medicine with the moral certainty that it will save her and kill her child? When we know principles clearly we can apply them boldly. I answer then with this important distinction: you can give such medicine as will act on her system, her organs, in a manner to save her life, and you may permit the sad effects which will indirectly affect the child; but you cannot injure the child directly as a means to benefit her indirectly; that would be using a bad means to obtain a good end.

Suppose, then, what is said to be a real case of occasional recurrence in obstetrical practice, namely, that a pregnant mother is seized with violent and unceasing attacks of vomiting, so that she must die if the vomiting be not stopped; and you, as well as the consulting physician called in, can discover no means of relieving the vomiting except by procuring an abortion, by relieving the womb of its living burden. Abortion is then the means used to stop the vomiting. Are you justified in using that means? Abortion is the dislodging of the child from the only place where it can live and where nature has placed it for that purpose. Therefore abortion directly kills the child, as truly as plunging a man under water kills the man. Can you thus kill the child to save the mother? You *cannot*. Neither in this case nor in any other case can you do evil that good may come of it.

You notice, gentlemen, that I lay great stress on, this principle that *the end can never justify the means*. It is an evident principle, which all civilized nations acknowledge. Its opposite, that the end justifies the means, is so odious that the practice of it is a black stamp of ignominy on any man or any set of men that would be guilty of it. The Catholic Church has, all through her course of existence, taught the maxim that the end cannot justify the means. She has impressed it on the laws and hearts of all Christian peoples. She inculcates it in the teachings of all her theologians and moral philosophers and in all her channels of education. And since we Jesuits are among her leading educators and writers, we have maintained that thesis in thousands of printed volumes, as firmly as I am maintaining it before you to-day. No Jesuit ever, nor any Catholic theologian or philosopher, has taught the contrary. And yet even such pretentious works as the "Encyclopædia Britannica" have carried all over the earth the slander that we teach the opposite maxim, that the end does justify the means, and the odious term *Jesuitry* has been coined to embody that slander.

Is it not strange then, very strange, that they who thus falsely accuse us are often the very men who will procure an abortion to save the mother's life, who will do wrong that good may come of it? And you find such men maintaining the lawfulness of abortion on the plea that the operation, whether licit or not, is a necessary means to obtain a good end.

IV. Gentlemen, if once you grant that grave reasons would justify abortion, there is no telling where you will stop in your career of crime. To-day, for instance, you are called to attend a mother, who, you think, must die if you do not bring on a miscarriage. You are urged to do it by herself and her husband, and perhaps by other physicians. There are money considerations too, and the possible loss of practice. Will you yield to the temptation? The next day you are visited by a most respectable lady; but she has been unfaithful to her marriage vow. The consequences of her fall are becoming evident. If her husband finds out her condition, he may wreak a terrible vengeance. Her situation is sadder than that of the sick mother of the preceding day. You can easily remove the proof of her guilt, we will suppose, and spare a world of woes. Will you withstand the temptation? The third day comes a young lady, a daughter of an excellent family; bright prospects lie before her; her parents' lives and happiness are wrapped up in that girl. But in an evil hour she has been led astray. Now she is with child. She begs, she implores you to save her from ruin, and her parents from despair. If you do not help her, some other Doctor or a quack will do it; but you could do it so much better. If you should have yielded on the two former occasions, if you have already stained your heart with innocent blood, will you now refuse? Where are you going to draw the line?

The passions of men are insatiate, even in modern society; the more you yield to them, the stronger grows their craving. Let me illustrate my meaning by a fact that happened a few years ago in Russia. It is just to our point. During a severe winter, a farmer, having his wife and children with him on a wagon, was driving through a wild forest. All was still as death except the howling of wolves in the distance. The howling came nearer and nearer. After a while a pack of hungry wolves was seen following in the track of the wagon. The farmer drove on faster, but they gained on him. It was a desperate race to keep out of their reach. At last they are just back of the wagon. What can be done? The next moment the wolves may jump on the uncovered vehicle. The children, horrified, crouch near their trembling mother. Suddenly the father, driven to despair, seizes one of the little children and flings it among the pack of wolves, hoping that by yielding them one he may save the rest. The hungry beasts stop a few moments to fight over their prey. But soon they are in hot pursuit again, fiercer because they have tasted blood. A second child is thrown to them, and after a while a third and a fourth.

Human society, gentlemen, in this matter of sacrificing fœtal life is as insatiable as a pack of hungry wolves. Woe to any one of you if he begins to yield to its cravings; there is no telling where he will stop. In proof of my statement, let me read to you an extract from a lecture on Obstetrics, delivered by Doctor Hodge, of Philadelphia, to the medical students of the University of Pennsylvania: "We blush while we record the fact, that, in this country, in our cities and towns, in this city where literature, science, morality, and Christianity are supposed to have so much influence; where all the domestic and social virtues are reported as being in full and delightful exercise; even here individuals, male and female, exist who are continually imbruing their hands and consciences in the blood of unborn infants; yea, even medical men are to be found who, for some trifling pecuniary recompense, will poison the fountains of life, or forcibly induce labor, to the certain destruction of the fœtus and not infrequently of the parent.

"So low, gentlemen, is the moral sense of the community on this subject, so ignorant are the greater number of individuals, that even mothers, in many instances, shrink not from the commission of this crime, but will voluntarily destroy their own progeny, in violation of every natural sentiment and in opposition to the laws of God and man. Perhaps there are few individuals in extensive practice who have not had frequent applications made to them by the fathers and mothers of unborn infants (respectable and polite in their general appearance and manners) to destroy the fruit of illicit pleasure, under the vain hope of preserving their reputation by this unnatural and guilty sacrifice.

"Married women, also, from the fear of labor, from indisposition to have the care, the expense, or the trouble of children, or some other motive equally trifling and degrading, have solicited that the embryo should be destroyed by their medical attendant. And when such individuals are informed of the nature of the transaction, there is an expression of real or pretended surprise that any one should deem that act improper, much more guilty; nay, in spite even of the solemn warnings of the physician, they will resort to the debased and murderous charlatan, who, for a piece of silver, will annihilate the life of the fœtus, and endanger even that of its ignorant or guilty mother.

"This low estimate of the importance of fœtal life is by no means restricted to the ignorant or to the lower classes of society. Educated, refined, and fashionable women, yea, in many instances, women whose lives are in other respects without reproach—mothers who are devoted with an ardent and self-denying affection to the children who already constitute the family—are perfectly indifferent concerning the fœtus *in utero*. They seem not to realize that the being within them is indeed *animate*, that it is in verity a *human* being, body and spirit; that it is of importance; that its value is inestimable, having reference to this world and the next. Hence they in every way neglect its interests. They eat and drink, they walk and ride; they will practise no self-restraint, but will indulge every caprice, every passion, utterly regardless of the unseen, unloved embryo....

"These facts are horrible, but they are too frequent and too true; often, very often, must all the eloquence and all the authority of the practitioner be employed; often he must as it were grasp the conscience of his weak and erring patient, and let her know, in language not to be misunderstood, that she is responsible to her Creator for the life of the being within her." (Wharton and Stillé's Med. Jur., Parturition, p. 92.)

Dr. Walter Channing, of Massachusetts, refers to the difficulty of obtaining a conviction for abortion, and adds: "I believe there has never been one in this State, this moral State by eminence, and perhaps in none is this crime more rife." ("Boston Med. and Surg. Journal," April, 1859, p. 135).

V. We have, then, proved, gentlemen, two important and pregnant principles: 1. That we can never directly procure abortion, and 2, that we can procure it indirectly in extreme cases; or rather that we can take such extreme measures in pressing danger as may likely result in abortion against our will.

While these principles are clear and undoubted, there are cases in which the right application of them is beset with great difficulties. These often occur in connection with what is called *ectopic* or *extra-uterine gestation*, namely, when the nascent human form lodges in some recess not intended by nature for its abode. Of late years, Dr. Velpeau, of Paris; Dr. Tait, of Birmingham, and many other eminent physicians have shown that cases of ectopic gestation are more numerous than had been supposed; one practitioner reports that he had attended fifty cases, another eighty-five.

1. We will first suppose the case of an interior growth occurring, the nature of which cannot be determined. It may be only a tumor, yet it may be the growth of a living fœtus. If no immediate crisis is feared, you will wait, of course, for further developments. If it proves to be a child, you will attempt no operation till it becomes viable at least. But suppose that fatal consequences are apprehended before the presence of a human being can be ascertained by the beating of the heart; suppose that delay would endanger the mother's life; and yet if you undertake to cut out the tumor, you may find it to contain fœtal life. In such urgent danger, can you lawfully perform

the operation? Let us apply our principles. You mean to operate on a tumor affecting one of the mother's organs. The consequences this may have for the child are not directly willed, but permitted. The four conditions mentioned before are hereby verified, under which the evil result, the death of the possible fœtus, may be lawfully permitted; namely: (*a*) You do not wish its death; (*b*) What you intend directly, the operation on the mother's organism, is good in itself; (*c*) The good effect intended, her safety, to which she has an undoubted right, overbalances the evil effect, the possible death of the child, whose right to life is doubtful, since its very existence is doubtful; now, a certain right must take precedence of a doubtful right of the same species; (*d*) The evil is not made the means to obtain the good effect (see "Am. Eccl. Rev.," Nov., 1893, p. 353). This last condition would not be verified if it were proposed, not to cut out the cyst, but to destroy its contents by an electric current. Then, it would seem, the fœtus itself, if there be one, would be directly attacked.

2. The case would present greater difficulties if the growth in question were *known* to contain a living fœtus. Such a case is discussed in all its details, with remarkable philosophical acumen, and in the light of copious information furnished by prominent members of the medical profession, in the pages of the "American Ecclesiastical Review" for November, 1893, pages 331–360. The participants in this interesting discussion are writers who enjoy a world-wide reputation for keenness of intellect and soundness of doctrine in philosophical and theological learning. They are not at all agreed as to the practical conclusion arrived at, and even those who agree to the same conclusion do so for different reasons. Three of them agree that in the case of a cyst known to contain a living embryo, when a rupture most probably fatal to mother and child is imminent, the abdominal section might be performed lawfully, the cyst opened and the child baptized before its certain death. Two of these justify this conclusion on the principle that the death of the child is then permitted only or indirectly intended; one

maintains that the killing of the embryo is then directly procured, but he considers that an embryo in a place not intended for it by nature is where it has no right to be, and therefore may be treated as an unjust aggressor upon the mother's life. At least one of the disputants condemns the operation as absolutely unlawful.

Gentlemen, when such authorities disagree, I would not presume to attempt a theoretic decision. But then we have this other principle practically to guide us, that in matters so very doubtful we need not condemn those who differ from our view, as long as they feel convinced that they are acting wisely and prudently. In Jurisprudence, reason must be our guide when it affords us evidence of the truth. But when our reason offers arguments on both sides of the question, so that we can arrive at no certain conclusion, then we act prudently by invoking the authority of wiser minds who make moral questions a speciality, and we are perfectly safe if we follow the best authority obtainable.

A Catholic physician has here a special advantage: for he has in cases of great difficulty the decisions of Roman tribunals, composed of most learned men, and renowned for the thoroughness of their investigations and the prudence of their verdicts, to serve him as guides and vouchers for his conduct. Although these tribunals claim no infallibility, yet they offer all the advantages that we look for, with regard to civil matters, in the decisions of our Supreme Court. These Roman courts have uniformly decided against any operation tending directly to the death of an innocent child ("Am. Eccl. Rev.," Nov., 1893, pp. 352, 353; Feb., 1895, p. 171).

Non-Catholics are, of course, not obliged to obey such pronouncements; yet, even for them, it cannot be injurious, but rather very useful, to know the views of so competent a court on matters of the most vital interest in their learned profession. This is the reason why the "Medical Record" has published of late so many articles on the teachings of

Catholic authorities with regard to craniotomy and abortion (see vol. xlvii. nos. 5, 9, 25; vol. xlviii. nos. 1, 2, 3, 4).

LECTURE IV.
VIEWS OF SCIENTISTS AND SCIOLISTS.

In my former lectures, gentlemen, I explained to you the principles condemnatory of craniotomy and abortion, viewing these chiefly from the standpoint of the ethical philosopher and the jurist. Not being a physician myself, I think it proper, on matters of so much importance, to quote here freely from a lecture delivered on this subject by a late professional gynecologist, an old experienced practitioner, who was for many years a professor of obstetrics in the St. Louis Medical College. I quote him with the more pleasure because of my personal acquaintance with him, and of the universal esteem for ability and integrity in which he was held by the medical profession.

Dr. L. Charles Boislinière, to whom I refer, had by his scientific acquirements and his successful practice, during forty years of his life, become, to a great extent, identified with the progress of the science of obstetrics in this country; and a few months before his late demise, he had published a useful work on "Obstetric Accidents, Emergencies, and Operations."

In 1892 he read, before the St. Louis Obstetrical and Gynecological Society, a lecture on the moral aspects of craniotomy and abortion, of which a considerable portion is very much to our present purpose. The Doctor herein clearly demonstrates that, in this matter at least, Ethics and Medical Science are to-day perfectly concordant. He says:

"The operation of craniotomy is a very old one. The ancients entertained the belief that, in difficult labors, the unborn child was an unjust aggressor against the mother, and must, therefore, be sacrificed to save her life.

"Hippocrates, Celsus, Avicenna, and the Arabian School invented a number of vulnerating instruments to enter and crush the child's cranium. With the advance of the obstetric art, more conservative measures were gradually adopted, such as the forceps, version, induction of premature labor, and, finally, Cesarean section.

"Cesarean section is reported to have been performed by Nicola de Falcon in the year 1491. Nufer, in 1500, and Rousset, in 1581, performed it a great many times, always successfully; so that, Scipio Murunia affirms, it was as common in France during that epoch as blood-letting was in Italy, where at that time patients were bled for almost every disease. However, a reaction soon followed, headed by Guillemau and Ambrose Pare, who had failed in their attempts at Cesarean section. In our days a marked change of opinion on this interesting and delicate question is rapidly taking place.

"With these advances in view, the question now is:

"*Are we ever justified in killing an unborn child in order to save the mother's life?*

"This is a burning question, and the sooner and more satisfactorily it is settled, the greater will be the peace to the medical mind and conscience.

"In answer to the question, I, at the outset, reply *No*, and claim that, under no conditions or circumstances, is it ever allowable to destroy the life of the child in order to increase the mother's chances of living. And the day may arrive when, by the law of the land, the act will be considered criminal and punished as such. In support of this opinion, and to illustrate this position, allow me to take a purely ethical and medico-legal view of the subject, and to relate to you a parallel case, as also the decision arrived at by the Lord Chief Justice of England, Judge Coleridge, than whom there is not a greater jurist living.

"The case is that of the British yacht 'Mignonette.' On July 5, 1884, the prisoners Dudley and Stevens, with one Brookes and the deceased, an English boy between 17 and 18 years of age, part of the crew of the 'Mignonette,' were cast away in a storm at sea 1,600 miles from the Cape of Good Hope, and were compelled to take to an open boat.

"They had no supply of water, no supply of food, and subsisted for twenty days on two pounds of turnips and a small turtle they had caught. They managed to collect a little rain-water in their oil-skin capes.

"On the eighteenth day, having been without food for seventeen days and without water for five days, the prisoners suggested that some one should be sacrificed to save the rest. Brookes dissented, and the boy, to whom they referred, was not consulted. On that day Dudley and Stevens spoke of their having families, and of their lives being more valuable than that of the boy. The boy was lying in the bottom of the boat, quite helpless, extremely weak and unable to make any resistance; nor did he assent to be killed to save the others. Dudley, with the assent of Stevens, went to the boy and, telling him that his time had come, put a knife into his throat and killed him. They fed upon his flesh for four days. On the fourth day the boat was picked up by a passing vessel, and the sailors were rescued, still alive but in a state of extreme prostration.

"The prisoners were carried to the port of Falmouth and committed for trial, the charge being murder. Their excuse was that, if they had not killed the boy and fed upon his flesh, there being no sail in sight, they would have died of starvation before being rescued. They said that there was no chance of saving their lives, except by killing some one for the others to eat. The prisoners were committed for murder and sentenced to death, but appealed to the mercy of the court, pleading ignorance. It was found by the verdict that the boy was incapable of resistance, and authorities were then quoted to prove that, in order to save your own life, you have the right to take the life of an unjust aggressor in self-defence—a principle the truth of which is universally admitted.

"But the evidence clearly showed that the defenceless boy was not an unjust aggressor against their lives, and, consequently, their only plea was that of expediency.

"In a chapter in which he deals with the exception created by necessity, Lord Hale, quoted by Justice Coleridge, thus expresses himself:

"'If a man be desperately assaulted and in peril of death, and cannot otherwise escape, except by killing an innocent person then present, the act will not acquit him of the crime and punishment of murder; for he ought rather to die himself than to kill an innocent.'

"In the case of two men on a plank at sea, which can only support one, the right of one occupant to throw the other overboard to save his own life, and in the instance of sailors, to save themselves, throwing passengers in the sea, are equally condemned by Lord Coleridge as unjustifiable homicide. So that under no circumstances is it allowable to kill an innocent aggressor to save your own life. I say *innocent* aggressor; but it is allowed, in self-defence, to kill, if necessary, an *unjust* aggressor against your life.

"This case is exactly analogous to that of the child lying helpless in its mother's womb. She causes its death by her consent to the act of her agent, the physician in attendance.

"Remark that Brookes, one of the sailors, dissented to the killing of the sailor-boy. This may happen in consultation, when one of the consultants does not admit the right to kill an unborn child. Please also remember that the sailor-boy lay helpless at the bottom of the boat when his assailants killed him to save their own lives.

"The child is not an unjust aggressor against the mother. It is placed in the womb without its consent and is defenceless. It is the mother who is, as it were, the aggressor from the obstacles caused by a deformed pelvis, tumors, etc.; and she has not the right to ask or consent to the killing of the child who does not attack her.

"Therefore, I repeat that the two cases are analogous; and if, as remarked by Justice Coleridge, murder was committed in the first instance, so is murder committed in the analogue. So, we see, the principal points of the opinion enunciated by the learned judge, and the principles therein laid down, can, with equal force, be applied to the non-justification of craniotomy, by which the life of a defenceless child is sacrificed to save the mother.

"Notice also that two of the perpetrators of the deed claimed that they had families, and that their lives were more valuable than that of the murdered boy. By craniotomists this reason or excuse is frequently given with much sentimentality to justify the killing of the child. The child, they say, has no social value, the mother is the idol of her husband, the pride of the household, often an ornament to society, the mother of living or possible children. Therefore, her life is more valuable than that of the unborn child. But who is to be the judge of the value of life? Were not Scipio Africanus, Manlius, was not Cæsar, from whom the very name of the operation, delivered by section from their mother's womb? The operation was familiarly known to Shakespeare, who tells us:

> 'Macduff was from his mother's womb
> untimely ripped.'

"There can never be a necessity for killing—except an unjust aggressor and in self-defence—unless the killing can be justified by some recognized excuse admitted by the law. In the case of the murdered sailor-boy, there was not such an excuse, unless the killing was justified by what has been called necessity. But, as stated above, there never is an excuse for killing an innocent aggressor, and the temptation to the act and its expediency is not what the law has ever called necessity. Nor is this to be regretted; for if in this case the temptation to murder and the expediency of the deed had been held by law as absolute defence of the deed, there would have been no guilt in the case. Happily this is not so. The plea of necessity once admitted might be made the legal cloak for unbridled passions and atrocious crimes, such as the producing of abortion, etc.

"As in the case of this young sailor, so in the killing of an unborn child, no such excuse can be pleaded; the unborn child cannot be the aggressor, no more so than the defenceless sailor-boy was.

"To preserve one's life is, generally speaking, a duty: but it may be the plainest duty, the highest duty, to sacrifice one's life. War is full of such instances in which it is not man's duty to live, but to die. The Greek and Latin authors contain many examples in which the duty of dying for others is laid down in most glowing and eloquent language.

"'*Dulce et decorum est pro patria mori,*' says Horace. Such was heathen ethics, and it is enough in a Christian country to teach that there is not always an absolute and unqualified necessity to preserve one's life.

"Thus, as a parallel case, is the situation of a woman in a difficult labor, when her life and that of her unborn child are in extreme danger. In this instance, it is the mother's duty to die rather than to consent to the killing of her child.

"In a subject of such delicacy and importance I have avoided all argument based upon the doctrines of any particular religion, and considered the subject upon its purely ethical and scientific basis. I am aware that I am taking a position quite at variance with that occupied by many men influenced by former teachings and prejudices.

"I respect the honest convictions of those opposed to the opinions presented in this paper. But it is hoped that thoughtful physicians will soon reconsider their views and adopt a more just and humane method of dealing with the rights of a living unborn child.

"As a hopeful sign, it is to be noticed that a gradual change is taking place in the opinions of the profession as to the propriety of performing craniotomy. Busey says: 'To state the issue plainly, the averment must be made that no conscientious physician would deliberately and wilfully kill a fœtus, if he believed that the act was a violation of the commandment "Thou shalt not kill."' It has been well said by Barnes, the ablest and most conservative defender of craniotomy, that 'it is not simply a question for medicine to decide. Religion and the civil law claim a preponderating voice. In the whole range of the practice of medicine, there arises no situation of equal solemnity.'

"Having thus far considered the subject from a purely ethical standpoint, I shall now present its scientific and practical aspect.

"Parvin says that the improved Cesarean section has given in Germany results so satisfactory that, possibly, the day is at hand when craniotomy upon the living fœtus will be very rarely performed, if done at all. Kinkead, a high English authority, states: 'To reduce the bulk of the child, or to extract it afterward through a pelvis of two and one-half or less conjugate diameter, is an operation of extreme difficulty, lengthy, requiring a very great experience, as far as the mother is concerned, requiring an amount of manual dexterity rarely to be acquired outside of a large city. While, on the other hand, the Cesarean section is an easy operation, capable of successful performance by any surgeon of ordinary skill.'

"Tait remarks that he 'feels certain that the decision of the profession will be, before long, to give up the performance of such operations as are destructive to the child, in favor of an operation that saves it, and subjects the mother to little more risk. The operation of Cesarean section, or the Porro amputation of the pregnant womb, will revolutionize the obstetric art, and in two years we shall hear no more of craniotomy; for the improved method will save more lives, and is far easier of performance. It is the easiest operation in abdominal surgery, and every country practitioner ought to be able, and always prepared, to do it.' So said Lawson Tait in 1888.

"I could quote many other authorities, showing the change that is taking place in the profession upon this important question. It is established by the consensus of professional opinion that craniotomy has been frequently performed in cases where delivery could have been safely accomplished by the forceps, turning, and even by the unaided power of nature (Busey); and there is no case known to him where a woman, on whom a section had been successfully performed, has refused to submit to its repetition in subsequent pregnancies. In Belgium the Cesarean section has been performed seven times on the same woman, and in Philadelphia three times. Doctor Bretoneaux, of Tours, has performed it six times on the same woman; and this woman his wife. 'The brutal epoch of craniotomy has certainly passed. The legitimate aspiration and tendency of science is to eliminate craniotomy on the living and viable child from obstetric practice.'—Barnes' words as quoted by Busey. Tyler Smith is in perfect accordance with Barnes. Barnes again writes: 'For the Cesarean section two very powerful arguments may be advanced. First, that the child is not sacrificed. Second, that the mother has a reasonable prospect of being saved.'

"Late reports of the Dublin Rotunda Hospital show that, in 3,631 cases of labor, craniotomy was performed only four times, and in three of these, positive diagnosis of the child's death was ascertained before the operation. In one of these cases the diagnosis was doubtful.

"More Madden, a celebrated obstetrician of forty years' experience, never performed it once.

"'The brilliant achievements in abdominal surgery give assurance that the Cesarean section is not only a legitimate operation, but one almost free from danger; also, that the tragic scenes heretofore witnessed in certain cases, in which the destruction of the child was resorted to, may be relegated to history (A. P. Clarke)."

Further on, Dr. Boislinière speaks more directly of abortion. He says:

"The principle once admitted that you are not justifiable in killing an innocent aggressor except in self-defence, equally prohibits any interference with early gestation.

"From the moment of conception the child is living. It grows, and what grows has life. *'Homo est qui homo futurus,'* says an ancient and high authority.

"Therefore, fœticide is not permissible at any stage of utero-gestation.

"The killing of the defenceless fœtus is sometimes done in cases of uncontrollable vomiting of pregnancy, in cases of tubal or abdominal gestation, and the killing of the fœtus is done by electricity, injections of morphine in the amniotic sac, the puncturing of that sac, etc.

"This practice is too lightly adopted by thoughtless or conscienceless physicians. This practice is much on the increase. I once heard a known obstetrician of the old school say: 'I would as lief kill, if necessary, an unborn child as a rat.' So much for the estimate he put on the value of human life! *O tempora! O mores!*

"Is it not time that this wanton 'massacre of the innocents' should cease?

"Without wishing to load this paper with elaborate statistics, I shall furnish the latest arrived at in the two operations of craniotomy and Cesarean section.

"In the combined reports of the clinics of Berlin, Halle, and Dresden, the maternal mortality in craniotomy was 5.8 per cent—of course, one hundred per cent of the children lost.

"In Cesarean section the maternal mortality was eight or eleven per cent; children's mortality, thirteen per cent.

"Caruso, the latest and most reliable statistician, not an optimist, sums up the results from the different clinics, and comes to the conclusion that craniotomy shows ninety-three and one one-hundredth mothers recover, Cesarean section eighty-nine and four one-hundredths.

"Caruso, therefore, concludes that craniotomy on the living child is to be superseded by Cesarean section. He says, therefore, that the mother has three chances out of four, and her child nine out of ten, for life.

"Leopold, as stated above, shows a much better result, viz.: ninety-five mothers saved out of one hundred by Cesarean section, a result equal that obtained in craniotomy."

You notice, gentlemen, that the eminent physician whom I have been quoting speaks with much indignation of the killing of the embryo, when he calls it a "massacre of the innocents." By this odious term we usually denote the massacre of the babes at Bethlehem, ordered by the infamous Herod to defend himself against the future aggression, as he imagined, of the new-born King of the Jews. A craniotomist would, no doubt, feel insulted at being compared with Herod. And yet, if we examine the matter closely, we shall find that the two massacres, Herod's and the craniotomist's, could only be defended by the same plea, that of necessity. "Necessity knows no law," writes Dr. Galloway, in his defence of craniotomy, to which I referred in a former lecture. "The same law," he writes in the "Medical Record" for July 27, 1895, "which lies at the basis of Jurisprudence in this respect justifies the sacrifice of the life of one person when actually necessary for the preservation of the life of another, when the two are reduced to such extremity that one or the other must die. This is the *necessitas non habet legem.*"

Did not Herod look on the matter just in that light? Expecting Christ to be, not a spiritual, but a temporal ruler, as the Jewish nation supposed at the time, he looked upon it as a case of necessity to sacrifice the lives of the innocents for his own preservation. "Necessity knows no law" was his principle. True, many had to die on that occasion to save one; but then he was a king. Anyhow, their death was necessary, and *necessitas non habet legem*; that settles it: Herod must not be blamed, on that principle. It is not even certain that, cruel as he was, he would have confessed, with the modern obstetrician, "I would as lief, if it were necessary, kill an unborn child as a rat."

Such sentiments, revolting as they are, and a disgrace to civilization, are the natural outcome of rash speculations about the first principles of morality.

The principle "*Necessitas non habet legem*" has indeed a true and harmless meaning when properly understood; it means that no law is violated when a man does what he is physically necessitated to do, and that no law can compel him to do more than he can do. Thus a disabled soldier cannot be compelled to march on with his regiment; necessity compels him to remain behind. In this sense the principle quoted is a truism; hence its universal acceptance. Applying the same principle in a wider sense, moralists agree that human law-givers do not, and in ordinary circumstances cannot, impose obligations the fulfilment of which requires extraordinary virtue. Even God Himself does not usually exact of men the performance of positive heroic acts. But no such plea can be urged to justify acts which God forbids by the natural law.[1] When necessity is used as a synonym for a "very strong reason," as it is in the plea of the craniotomist, then it is utterly false that very strong reasons for doing an act cannot be set aside by a divine law to the contrary; what is wrong in itself can never become right, even though the strongest arguments could be adduced in its favor. It would be doing wrong that good may come of it, or making the end justify the means. Such principles may be found in the code of tyrants and criminals, but should not be looked for in the code of Medical Jurisprudence.

[1] See this point more fully treated in the Author's "Moral Philosophy," Book. I. c. ii., "The Morality of Human Acts."

There is but one plea left, I believe, on which, of late years, it is sometimes attempted to justify the murder of little children. It is the plea of some evolutionists who maintain that the infant has not yet a true human soul. I should not deign to consider this theory if it were not that I find it seriously treated by a contributor to the "Medical Record," in an article which, on September 4, 1895, concluded a long discussion on craniotomy published in that learned periodical.

The writer of this article asserts: "Procuring the death of the fœtus to save the life of the mother is, I am sure, to be defended on ethical grounds." And here is the way he attempts to defend it: "We may safely assume," he argues, "that the theory of evolution is the best working hypothesis in every branch of natural science. We are learning through Herbert Spencer and all late writers on ethics and politics, that the same principle will best explain the facts" (p. 395).

I do not deny that a certain school of scientists is trying to rewrite all history and all Ethics and Jurisprudence. But the writer strangely misstates the case when he says that "all great writers on ethics and politics" agree with Mr. Spencer. Besides a multitude of others, Lord Salisbury for one, has clearly shown of late that the school of agnostic evolutionists is coming to grief; it has had its short day, and it is now setting below the horizon of ignominy and subsequent oblivion. The writer of the article in question does not attempt to prove the evolution theory; therefore I need not stop to disprove it. But he makes the following application of it to our subject—an application so shocking to humanity and so revolting to common sense that, if it is logical, it is by itself sufficient to refute the whole theory of Mr. Spencer and his school.

He argues that, if that theory be admitted, it must necessarily follow that, while the human embryo is from the first alive, it is not a human being until it has developed and differentiated to such a point as corresponds to that point at the birth of the race where the animal becomes a man. "I am sure," he adds, "I do not know when that occurred in the past, and I do not know at what point it occurs in the individual.... In inquiring for that distinct feature which distinguishes the man from the animal, I find none but mentality. If we wait for distinct mentality to appear in the development of the individual, it would be some time after birth."

According to this reasoning a child is not known to be a human being till some time after its birth. And this is not uttered by some speculative philosopher in his closet, but by a medical practitioner on his daily rounds, tools in hand, as it were, to carry out his theory and break the skulls of any and all luckless babes that may come in his way in the exercise of what he calls his legitimate practice. How long after birth the child remains without becoming a human being, he does not pretend to know; they remain non-human till they manifest mental action. Till then, not being human, he assigns them no human rights—no rights at all which we are conscientiously obliged to respect. Herod may have been right after all when he appointed the term of two years old and under as the limit of the butchery at Bethlehem. The writer pretends to lessen the horror inspired by his theory by referring to some restrictions of canon law. But what do he and his like care about canon law? He would be the first to scout the idea of letting canon law limit his freedom of action and speculation.

What would be the real results in practical life if we were to accept as rules of conduct these rash theories of agnostic philosophers and infidel scientists? Justly does the writer proceed to say: "I am well aware that the idea arouses antagonism and inflammatory denunciation in some minds." Certainly it does. He adds: 'That it [the idea] will prove to be the true one, however, depends only on the truth of the general theory of development.' If this be the logical consequence of evolution, or Darwinism, as he calls it, then all the worse for Darwinism. Society cannot get along on a theory that begets such principles of action; the more so since, in Spencer's and in Darwin's system, the human soul, even in grown persons, is only a material modification of the body and perishes with it in death. Hence there would be no responsibility after death. On this theory the physician is only a lump of very curiously evolved matter; he, too, like the embryo, is without an immortal soul, is not a free being, and therefore is incapable of having rights or duties.

Before we remodel our codes of Ethics and Jurisprudence by the admission into them of such destructive and revolutionary principles, we shall at least be allowed to challenge these aggressors and ask solid proof of their rash innovations. We may address to them the wise words uttered against similar speculators by one of the most logical of modern reasoners, the illustrious Cardinal Newman. "Why may not my first principles contest the prize with yours? they have been longer in the world, they have lasted longer, they have done harder work, they have seen rougher service. You sit in your easy-chairs, you dogmatize in your lecture-rooms, you wield your pens: it all looks well on paper; you write exceedingly well; there never was an age in which there was better writing, logical, nervous, eloquent, and pure,—go and carry it out in the world. Take your first principles, of which you are so proud, into the crowded streets of our cities, into the formidable classes which make up the bulk of our population: try to work society by them. You think you can; I say you cannot; at least you have not as yet, it is to be seen if you can.... My principles, which I believe to be eternal, have at least lasted eighteen hundred years; let yours last as many months.... These principles have been the life of nations; they have shown they could be carried out; let any single nation carry out yours" ("Present Position of Catholics in England." p. 293).

Gentlemen, let no one trifle with the principles of Ethics and Jurisprudence; human society cannot get along without them. Morality is the heart of civilization: its principles are the life-blood, which it sends forth to feed and warm and strengthen and beautify all the organs of its earthly frame. A flesh-wound may be healed, a bone may be set, it may knit and grow vigorous again; but you must not puncture the heart, nor attempt to change the natural channels of the circulating blood, under the penalty of having a corpse on your hands. So you must respect the eternal laws that direct the current of man's moral actions, the principles of Ethics and Jurisprudence.

LECTURE V.
VENEREAL EXCESSES.

In the opening lecture of this course, I remarked to you, gentlemen, that the scope of Medical Jurisprudence is much wider than that of Medical Law. It embraces many subjects of which human laws take no cognizance, and in particular such vicious actions as do not violate the rights of others, but are injurious to those only who practise them. They undermine the health and shorten the lives of the guilty parties, and bring in their train diseases the most destructive and often the most incurable. It is the physician's beneficent task to lessen the weaknesses and sufferings of the body, and to prolong human life in well-preserved vigor to a green old age. It is not the least important part of his valuable services to provide for the sound and vigorous propagation of the human race to future generations. Of this propagation of our race, of the laws which govern it, and of the criminal abuses by which these laws are violated, I am to treat in this present lecture. My subject is "Venereal Excesses."

I. If a physician's purpose were only to make money, his task would then be to multiply diseases and infirmities; he would then be as great a curse to mankind as he is really intended to be a blessing; and an immense blessing he will be to his fellow-men if he studies to remove even the remote causes of diseases and untimely deaths. He can do so in a variety of ways and not the least by providing against sexual excesses and abuses. These are a copious fountain of ill to humanity. A host of diseases, such as tuberculosis, diabetes, cardial and nervous affections, epilepsy, hysteria, general debility, weaknesses of sight, languor and general worthlessness, hypochondria, weakness and total loss of reason, and, in married life, impotence and sterility are some of the effects of venereal excesses. Any excitement of the sexual passion before the body has received its full development is more or less injurious to its welfare; and all excesses or unnatural indulgence of it at any period of life is pregnant with deplorable consequences. Now, such evil practices are too much overlooked by many physicians; yet it is certain that thousands of patients might, by timely warning on these matters, be saved from unspeakable mental and physical sufferings. To give sensible and intelligible directions on a subject as delicate as it is important in medical practice, it will be necessary to enter into some scientific details.

The passion which prompts to sexual intercourse is altogether natural in itself, and, as such, intended by the Creator to be indulged in at the right time and in the proper manner. It is the stimulus which He has provided for the propagation of the human race. If the stimulus is strong at times, this too is a special effect of His wisdom; because without a powerful prompting of this kind, most men would shirk the burden of married life, just as very many would not care to toil if they had no hunger and thirst and other bodily wants to satisfy.

But though all these cravings are useful and even indispensable to mankind, all of them need the regulation of reason. When they are indulged immoderately or in unnatural ways, they become most copious sources of bodily diseases, of mental disorders, and moral degradation. Every one knows how the passion of drink, when abused, proves the ruination of millions; excessive eating, too, injures the systems of countless people. But no animal passion is more liable to become disorderly, none needs more firm control and habitual watchfulness, than the passion of lust. Reason dictates that it should be indulged for no other purpose than that for which the Creator has made it, namely, marital intercourse. I say *marital* and not merely sexual intercourse; for outside of married life all nations have always condemned its indulgence.

Besides, it is only in the married state that the children, which are the fruit of such intercourse, can be properly educated. To generate a race of young barbarians is certainly not the purpose of the sexual relations. Children must not be begotten unless they can be properly raised, in a manner worthy of their noble destiny. Now, it is only in the married state, in the family or domestic society, that they can be thus educated. They need the tender hand of a mother to supply their material wants; they need the manly care of a devoted father to provide the necessaries of life, his firm hand to break their wanton wills, and his wise direction to set them well on the road to temporal and eternal happiness. Therefore, no one has the right to beget or to bear children except in marital life. Now, the sexual passion is to be exercised only in connection with its proper object, the procreation of children and the fostering of such mutual love between husband and wife as is conducive to domestic happiness. Therefore this passion is to be kept under careful and rational constraint. This the law of morality requires; all nations have ever exacted that this passion shall be subject to established rules; no free-love has ever been tolerated where there was the least pretence to civilization, and I do not know that it was ever permitted even among barbarians.

Even the distant approach that Mormonism made towards free-love has been absolutely condemned and repressed by the common-sense of the American people, as incompatible with civilization. In fact, all history testifies that the true civilization of any race or country rises or falls with the restraints imposed on the passion of lust; no polygamous nation has ever been more than half-civilized. The greatness of Rome and Greece decayed when the laws of social purity declined; and in our own day the immorality of what is called "the social evil" is the darkest stain on modern civilization.

And what we say of civilization or social soundness, the soundness of the body politic, applies in a great measure to individual soundness, the health of every person's mind and body. Personal purity promotes health and vigor, it lends beauty to form, gives a keen edge to the intellect, adds energy and brings success to manhood, and prepares for enduring and honored old age. Venereal excesses, on the contrary, undermine the vigor of the constitution, bring on a host of bodily infirmities, exhaust the system before the proper time, debauch and degrade the mind and will, and prepare their victims for an early grave or a decrepit old age.

II. But how can a passion so ardent be properly restrained? In particular, what can a physician do to prevent the manifold injuries which, if not properly controlled, it will bring to his patients? These are practical questions directly to our purpose.

The first requisite for all effective action is to have correct knowledge and strong convictions on a subject. No one will check a passion with firmness if he have a lingering doubt as to whether, after all, he is strictly bound to restrain it. As a man's mind matures, at least if his mind be upright and not distorted by the strain of a ruling passion, he understands more and more thoroughly that his perfection consists and his highest interests lie in obeying at all times the law of reason, in maintaining his specific dignity of a rational being, and not allowing himself to be controlled by passion, the ruling power of brute animals. Besides, he becomes aware in various ways of the evil results of immoral practices, and he sees many reasons to keep his passions in check. But young people have neither such experience nor such information, and they are not always wise enough to understand the imperative dictates of self-restraint. And yet it is often in early years, while body and mind are in the period of development, that the most serious injury is done to the constitution and to the character by the indulgence of carnal pleasures. Habits are then engendered which become a real slavery; so that later in life when there arises a sincere desire to stop such disgraceful practices, there is a feeling of impotence to resist temptations which by one's own fault have become a second nature.

What then can be done with the young? They must early and authoritatively be told of the wrong, the sin of base self-indulgence, and of every practice that leads to it. If a beginning of immorality is discovered in a child, it must be plainly told and emphatically warned of the serious consequences involved. The child's mother is, as a rule, the best guide and director in infancy. Later on, the Doctor has frequent chances to do so; it comes from him with better grace than from others; and his warning is likely to be minded, because it is clear that he knows and ought to know what he is talking about with regard to bodily consequences. Yet it is always a matter of delicacy; and great care should be taken lest, while pointing out the evil, there be also a stimulus added to a prurient curiosity.

Much good sense is required in any given case to decide whether more good or more evil is likely to result from the warning; in doubt of success, it is better to leave the matter alone.

> "Where ignorance is bliss
> 'Tis folly to be wise."

The safest way of repressing the passion of lust is the provision that an all-wise Providence supplies in Religion, in which God authoritatively forbids all immoral action and even all immoral coveting or desire. Positive dogmatic teaching on this subject is required, especially with the young. You cannot argue with them on this matter as you can with grown people. That is one reason why religious teaching should permeate early education. The Decalogue should be the back-bone of a child's training: and it should be proposed on the authority of God, and explained so as to check not only sinful acts, but also covetings, prurient curiosity, improper reading, immodest looks and thoughts, in a word, whatever paves the way to the walks of sin. The greatest of teachers has Himself laid down the law in this matter: it must be proposed as coming from His divine lips, as it did: "I say to you that whosoever shall look on a woman to lust after her has already committed adultery with her in his heart" (St. Matt. v. 28). The lesson is enforced by these words of the great Apostle: "Neither fornicators, nor adulterers, nor the effeminate ... shall possess the kingdom of God" (1 Cor. vi. 9, 10).

True, the child will not realize the full import of such lessons; but he will understand it in due time; and already in early years he will be warned against indulging his nascent passions. It is well that the conscience should be early awakened in this matter; for the more this passion is indulged, the more it craves for further indulgence till it becomes almost uncontrollable.

III. No possible evil to any individual man or woman can result from the firm control that one may acquire over the passion of lust. On the contrary, if it should be controlled all through life, this would only add to a man's strength of mind, firmness of will, soundness of body, and length of life. For in the school of morality, in which every Physician should be educated, the leading principle is: "Contraries are cured by contraries," "*Contraria contrariis curantur.*" On this principle, lust is most efficiently controlled by aiming, at least in youth, at total abstinence from its indulgence. You know that, in the Catholic Church, priests and religious lead a single life, and pledge themselves for life to practise the most perfect control of the sexual passion. What do you think is the result of their total abstinence on this point with regard to their length of days? As a rule their life is much longer, in normal circumstances, than that of the other learned professions. Here are a few proofs. In France, during the twenty years from 1823 to 1843, 750 priests died in the diocese of Paris. Of these only 200 were under sixty years old; there were 554 between sixty and seventy years old, 448 over seventy, and 177 over eighty. Again, of 202 Carmelite nuns who died in a large convent of Paris, Dr. Descuret, the attending physician, states that 82 had lived over seventy years, 23 over eighty years. Most

Trappists and Carthusians die of scarcely any other sickness than old age. All young people who aspire to the clerical or religious profession learn from their early years the holiness and the loveliness of purity. Our Church effects this result by placing before their youthful imaginations the most perfect of patterns of virtue, the infant Saviour, the virgin Mother, the boy saints Aloysius and Stanislaus, the maidens Agatha and Cecilia, and a whole phalanx of Christian heroes and heroines.

I dwell the more willingly on this subject, gentlemen, because, besides protecting modesty in your young patients generally, it may fall to the lot of some of you, in the course of your professional careers, to be attending physicians to religious houses; and you will then appreciate the delicacy of the flowers of virtue that bloom beneath the shadow of the sanctuary. Certainly even there you may happen to find isolated cases of infidelity to duty; for human nature is not angelic nature; but in such abodes it comes near to it, at least for the vast majority.

IV. On the other hand, what sad havoc does not the sexual passion play where it is precociously developed and wantonly indulged. Dr. H. Fournier, one of the most eminent physicians of Paris, says: "There is not a vice more fatal to the conservation of man than masturbation." This unfortunate habit is sometimes acquired by very little boys and girls. Foolish or vicious nurses may bring it on by handling young children most indelicately. This is one of the many reasons why none but virtuous servants and nurses should be employed by wise parents and physicians. In later years, children often learn this degrading and most injurious vice from their depraved companions, some of whom seem even to regard the practice of it as a manly accomplishment. When habitually indulged in, it produces on the health and the strength of the constitution effects the most deplorable. Even the intellect is liable to become thereby enfeebled, a want of virility is exhibited both in the body and in the mind of its victims; then follows a loss of ambition and self-control. "When this morbid passion gets control of a person," writes an experienced practitioner in medicine, "it is as though an unclean spirit had entered, subdued the will, weakened the moral forces, enfeebled the intellectual faculties, lessened the power to resist temptation, and overcome every obstacle opposed to its gratification. Even while the intellect is still clear, and the sense of wrong keen, the individual is a slave to this morbid impulse." Though the baneful effects may not always affect the physical health of the victim, the unfortunate practice very often engenders in boys and girls tendencies which in later years lead to all the miseries conspicuous in houses of debauch and infamy. But I need not dwell on consequences that belong to pathology rather than to Jurisprudence.

V. Confining myself to my sphere of what is morally right or wrong, I must be permitted to point out some gross violations of duty in some members of your honored profession. There are physicians so reckless of consequences and of principles alike as to advise at times the practice of illicit sexual intercourse. Let them beware; they are doing a very unwise and guilty act. Even if an immoral practice should save a human life, it may not be indulged, on the principle which must be by this time very familiar to your ears, that the end does not justify the means. And besides no good result can be expected from what is contrary to the law of nature and of nature's God. It was to punish sins of the flesh that the Deluge was sent, which destroyed nearly the whole human race. "All flesh had corrupted its way," says the sacred historian. It was to punish unlawful indulgence of lust that Sodom and Gomorrha were destroyed by fire from heaven; and the memory of these guilty cities is preserved in the very name of Sodomy. Onan, as the same sacred volume relates (Gen. xxxviii), performed the marriage act in a manner to frustrate it of its legitimate purpose, the generation of children, and the Lord slew him; and his sin is to this very day branded with his name and called Onanism. And yet in Christian lands physicians are found who will at times dare to recommend such practices to their patients.

On the occasions mentioned, God punished the guilty miraculously; but that is not His usual way. He has so contrived our natures that sins committed against His laws in our bodies ordinarily bring a part of their punishment in their train, not the less certain because slower in its operation than a miracle would be. All the venereal diseases are there to act as earthy ministers of Heaven's justice, anticipating, and often mercifully averting, the punishments of the future world.

VI. Besides private and secret tortures of body and mind, a public and most deplorable calamity has descended of late on our own vigorous young nation, as well as on some older lands, threatening in the not distant future the extinction of many of its most esteemed families and of what was, not long ago, a vigorous stock. The following article by Dr. Walter Lindley, Professor of Gynecology in the University of Southern California, will explain the matter better than my words could do. It was read in Los Angeles at a meeting of the Southern Californian Medical Society in June, 1895, and is printed in the "N. Y. Medical Journal" of August 17 of the same year (pp. 211 and following). It is headed "American Sterility;" I will quote freely from it:

"The obstetrician finds his vocation disappearing among the American women from the face of the earth.

"It is a fact that the American family with more than one or two children is the exception. From the records of six generations of families in some New England towns, it was found that the families comprising the first generation had on an average between eight and ten children; the next three generations averaged about seven to each family; the fifth generation less than three to each family. The generation now on the stage is not doing so well as that. In Massachusetts the average family numbers less than three persons. In 1885 the census of Massachusetts disclosed that 71.28 per cent of the women of that State were childless. The census of 1885 in the State of New York shows that twenty-five per cent of the women of that State are childless, fifty per cent average less than one child, and seventy-five per cent average only a trifle over one child.

"Southern California has fully as dark a record as New England—that is, in the family where the man and wife are American-born. It goes without saying that the medical profession in this country is composed to a great extent of typical progressive Americans, and I ask you to make mental statistics of the children in the families of the physicians in Southern California, and you will find very few of them containing more than two.

"Had the Rev. T. R. Malthus lived in the United States to-day, he would never have argued about the danger of over-population, as he did in his interesting volume on 'The Principles of Population.'"

After quoting the views of Plato, Aristotle, and Lycurgus, Dr. Lindley continues: "In Southern California there are, it is true, many children, but the average American family is very small.

"As I sat writing this an evening or two ago, I jotted down the names of twenty-five families of my acquaintance in Los Angeles, taking them as fast as I thought of them. The list was composed entirely of professional and business men ranging in age from thirty-five to fifty. All had been married quite a number of years. The result of my memorandum was that in these twenty-five families there were but eighteen children. These families were wholly unselected, and are about the average Protestant American families outside the rank of laborers.

"What are the causes of this small proportion of children? Disease, preventives of conception, and abortion form the trinity of responsibility in this grave condition. It is true that the first cause (disease) results in many women being barren, but I believe that you will agree with me that the last two causes, preventives of conception and abortion, are the two chief causes.

"The A. P. A. might find food for thought by investigating the infrequency of criminal abortion in Catholic families in the United States. It is the Protestant or agnostic American who too often uses one of the preventives of conception." (Here the Doctor refers to a foot-note in which he says: "I write this opinion as a Protestant, and should be glad to learn that it is not well founded.") He continues: "If, through inadvertence, pregnancy should occur, then an abortion is in order. Disease and poverty and war and accident all work together to keep down the population, but we are overcoming these. Plagues and pestilences are rare. The number who die of starvation in California is very small, while war has played but a small part. Through the diffusion of the laws of sanitation, improved dietary, and advanced therapeutics, the longevity of man is increasing, but the American woman's aversion to child-bearing is blighting our civilization, and can be well named the twentieth-century curse. In this aversion the woman frequently echoes the wish of the husband.

"A large proportion of the American young women who marry do so with the determination that they will have no children. They are abetted in this notion by many elderly women. The cure for this terrible sentiment is education. The home, the press, the schoolroom, and the pulpit should be centres for reviving the ancient idea of the nobility of motherhood. The physician should not underestimate his influence.

"By constantly bearing in mind the danger of the present tendencies, he can do much to change the current. Let us hope that we shall again see the day when thoughtful motherhood shall be considered the highest function of womanhood, and to shirk this natural duty will be deemed a disgrace."

Gentlemen, it would be easy to prove that this testimony of Dr. Lindley is not that of an exceptional witness, or a piece of special pleading; but it is the acknowledged conviction of the medical profession generally, confirmed by the last United States Census, and in fact not questioned, to my knowledge, by any weighty authority. As early as 1857, Dr. H. B. Storer, an eminent physician of Boston, startled the community by publishing two books on this subject, entitled: "Criminal Abortion. Why not?—A Book for Every Woman"; "Is it I?—A Book for Every Man." Soon after, Rev. John Todd, a Protestant minister of Pittsfield, Massachusetts, published a work styled "Serpents in the Dove's Nest," all which works and a multitude of others tell the same tale of woe regarding the increase of child-destroying crimes in New England, chiefly among the old stock peculiarly called Americans. Dr. Nathan Allen, of Lowell, Massachusetts, in his treatises, "Changes in the New England Population" and "The New England Family," gives overwhelming testimony. "Harper's Magazine" (quoted by the "Catholic World" for April, 1869) remarks: "We are shocked at the destruction of human life on the banks of the Ganges, but here in the heart of Christendom fœticide and infanticide are extensively practised under the most aggravating circumstances." We Catholics are not personally interested in this matter; but the good of our fellow-men and chiefly our fellow-countrymen calls for the earnest exertion of us all to stop this dreadful evil. All the works I have referred to exempt Catholics from the blame pronounced; the "Harper's Magazine" article referred to expressly says: "It should be stated that believers in the Roman Catholic faith never resort to any such practices; the strictly Americans are almost alone guilty of such crimes." This matter is fully explained in a recent work called "Catholic and Protestant Countries Compared," by Rev. Alfred Young, C.P., ch. xxxii.

VII. Now, gentlemen, I am very much afraid that while physicians as a body abhor all such murders and openly condemn them, many do not show much repugnance to allow, and even sometimes to suggest, such onanistic intercourse among married people as shall prevent the possibility of conception. For instance, if it happens that a young mother suffers much in her first confinement, at once the suggestion is made that a second parturition may prove fatal. From that moment regular intercourse is dreaded. Either onanism is habitually practised, or the husband becomes a frequent visitor to dens of infamy, where to where to save his wife's health, he encourages a traffic that leads multitudes of wretched girls to a premature and miserable death. Every one despises those outcasts of society; but are not the men who patronize them just as guilty? Probably enough, if the imprudent suggestion about dangers of a second child-bearing had not been made by the Doctor, the young wife might have become the happy mother of a numerous family of healthy children. For we must trust in Divine Providence. If a husband and wife do their conscientious duty, there is a God that provides for them and their family more liberally than for the birds of the air and the lilies of the field. And if He should so dispose that the worst should befall, well, such temporal clangers and sufferings as attend child-bearing are the lot of woman-kind, just as the dangers and hardships of the battlefield, the mine, the factory, the forest, and the prairie are the lot of the men.

The man who shirks his duty to family or country is a coward; women, as a rule, are brave enough in their own line of duty, and patiently submit to God's sentence pronounced in Paradise, "I will multiply thy sorrows and thy conceptions, in sorrow shalt thou bring forth children" (Gen. iii. 16), just as they have to submit to the words immediately following: "Thou shalt be under thy husband's power, and he shall have dominion over thee."

Certainly, the husband of a delicate woman ought to spare her strength and restrain his passion, but not at the sacrifice of morality; and Doctors ought to be very careful not to cause false or exaggerated alarms, and thus make themselves to some extent responsible for untold moral evils. They should remember that, as a rule, the raising of a family is the principal purpose of a married life. The happiness and virtue of the parties concerned depend chiefly on the faithful performance of this duty. How sad is the lot of those—and they are many—who undertook in early years of married life to prescribe a narrow limit to the number of their children; they had one or two, and they would have no more, and for this purpose criminally thwarted the purposes of nature. Then comes death and snatches away their solitary consolation: and they spend their old age childless and loveless, in mutual upbraidings and unavailing regrets.

How different is the lot of those aged couples—and they were many of yore, and are yet in various nations—who are like patriarchs amid their crowds of children and grandchildren and great-grandchildren, dwelling in mutual love and as if in a moral paradise where all domestic virtues bloom!

VIII. True, such families are usually the outcome of moderately early marriages; and many Doctors nowadays disapprove of such unions as an evil. A moral evil they certainly are not; and the physical evils sometimes attending them must, I think, be traceable to a variety of causes; for such evils are certainly not inseparable from early marriages. As to their moral advantages, Mr. Wm. E. H. Lecky, in his "History of European Morals," writes of the Irish people in particular: "The nearly universal custom of early marriages among the Irish peasantry has alone rendered possible that high standard of female chastity, that intense and jealous sensitiveness respecting female honor, for which, among many failings and some vices, the Irish race have long been pre-eminent in Europe" (v. i. p. 146). And that he does not confine his statement to female chastity is evident from what he adds farther on: "There is no fact in Irish history more singular than the complete and, I believe, unparalleled absence among the Irish priesthood of those moral scandals which in every Continental country occasionally prove the danger of vows of celibacy. The unsuspected purity of the Irish priesthood in this respect is the more remarkable, because, the government of the country being Protestant, there is no special inquisitorial legislation to insure it, because of the almost unbounded influence of the clergy over their parishioners, and also because, if any just cause of suspicion existed, in the fierce sectarianism of Irish public opinion it would assuredly be magnified. Considerations of climate are quite inadequate to explain this fact; but the chief cause is, I think, sufficiently obvious. The habit of marrying at the first development of the passions has produced among the Irish peasantry, from whom the priests for the most part spring, an extremely strong feeling of the iniquity of irregular sexual indulgence, which retains its power even over those who are bound to perpetual celibacy" (p. 147). No one will say, I believe, that the custom of early marriages in Ireland has any injurious effects on the health of either parents or children. Nor need it necessarily have such effects on those of our American young men and women who lead regular lives and are not enfeebled by unnatural vices or demoralized by dainty food and luxurious manners.

A wise physician has many proper ways of providing for the health and strength of both parents and children without advocating practices which are a snare for innocence. Let him insist with all his patients on the cultivation of healthful habits for the family and the individual; wholesome and not over-delicate food; moderation in eating and drinking; regular and manly exercise, especially in the open air; early hours for retiring and rising. But, above all—and this is directly to our present purpose—let him show the greatest regard for the laws of morality, the main support of individual and social happiness. His views upon such matters, manifested alike in his conduct and his conversation, but especially in his management of cases involving the application of moral principles, will go far to influence the community in which he moves. His task is to be a blessing to his fellow-men, a source of happiness and security to individuals and to society.

LECTURE VI.
THE PHYSICIAN'S PROFESSIONAL RIGHTS AND DUTIES.

Gentlemen, so far I have explained the duties which the physician has in common with all other men, and which arise directly from the natural law independently of any civil legislation. The natural law requires the Doctor to respect the life of the unborn child, thus forbidding craniotomy and abortion. It also obliges him to protect his patients from the baneful effects of venereal excesses. Over these matters human law has no control, except that it may and ought to punish such overt acts as violate the rights of individuals, or seriously endanger the public welfare.

We shall now consider the physician's natural rights and duties in regard to matters which civil and criminal legislation justly undertake to regulate. One of the chief functions of civil authority is to provide for the observance of contracts. Now, the physician in his professional services acts under a double contract, a contract with the state and a contract with his individual patients. By accepting his diploma of M.D. from the college faculty, and indirectly from the civil authority, he makes at least an implicit contract with the state, by which he receives certain rights conditioned on his performance of certain duties. In offering his services to the public, he also makes an implicit contract with his patients by which he obliges himself to render them his professional services with ordinary skill and diligence on condition of receiving from them the usual compensation.

I. The chief rights conferred on him by the state are these:

1. Protection against all improper interference with his professional ministrations.
2. Protection for his professional career by the exclusion of unauthorized practitioners.
3. Immunity from responsibility for evil consequences that may result without his fault from his medical or surgical treatment of patients.
4. Enforcement of his right to receive due compensation for his professional services.

These rights are not granted him arbitrarily by the state; they are founded in natural justice, but made definite and enforced by human legislation. Take, for an example, his right to receive due compensation for his services. This right was not recognized by the old Roman law in the case of advocates and physicians, nor by the common law of England until the passing of the Medical Act in 1858. Surgeons and apothecaries could receive remuneration for their services, but not physicians. These were presumed to attend their patients for an *honorarium* or honorary, that is, a present given as a token of honor.

Certainly, if Doctors by common agreement waived their right to all compensation, or agreed to be satisfied with any gift the patient might choose to bestow, they would be entitled to honor for their generosity; but they are not obliged to such conduct on the principles of natural justice. For by nature all men are equal, and therefore one is not obliged, under ordinary circumstances, to work for the good of another. If he renders a service to a neighbor, equity or equality requires that the neighbor shall do a proportionate good to him in return. Thus the equality of men is the basis of their right to compensation for services rendered. The physician's right to his fee is therefore a natural right, and on his patient rests the natural duty of paying it. Not to pay the Doctor's bill is as unjust as any other manner of stealing.

As to the amount of compensation to which the Doctor is justly entitled, Ewell's "Medical Jurisprudence" remarks: "By the law of this country, all branches of the profession may recover at law a reasonable compensation for their services, the amount of which, unless settled by law, is a question for the jury; in settling which the eminence of the practitioner, the delicacy and difficulty of the operation or of the case, as well as the time and care expended, are to be considered. There is no limitation by the common law as to the amount of such fees, provided the charges are reasonable. The existence of an epidemic does not, however, authorize the charge of an exorbitant fee.

"A medical man can also recover for the services rendered by his assistants or students, even though the assistant is unregistered; it is not necessary that there should be any agreed specified price, but he will be allowed what is usual or reasonable.

"It is not the part of the physician's business, ordinarily, to supply the patient with drugs; if he does so he has a right to compensation therefor. If the agreement is "No cure, no pay," he cannot, however, even recover for medicines supplied, if the cure is not effected. His right to recover for professional services does not depend upon his effecting a cure, or upon his service being successful, unless there is a special agreement to that effect; but it does depend upon the skill, diligence, and attention bestowed" (pp. 3 and 4).

Further details on this point belong more properly to the lecturer on Medical Law. We are now concerned with the principles underlying special legislation. The main principle regulating all compensation is that there shall be a sort of equality between the services rendered and the fee paid for them. Ignorant people sometimes find fault with the amount charged as a Doctor's fee. There may, of course, be abuses by excess; but men have no right to complain that a Doctor will ask as much for a brief visit as a common laborer can earn in a day. This need not seem unfair if it be remembered that the physician had to prepare, during many years of primary, intermediate, and professional studies, before he could acquire the knowledge necessary to write a brief prescription. Besides, it may be that his few minutes' visit is the only one that day; and yet he has a right to live in decent comfort on his profession together with those who depend on him for support.

We must, however, remember, on the other hand, that excessive fees are nothing else than theft; for theft consists in getting possession of another's property without just title. The following rules of Dr. Ewell are sensible and fair:

"The number of visits required must depend upon the circumstances of each particular case, and the physician is regarded by the law as the best and proper judge of the necessity of frequent visits; and, in the absence of proof to the contrary, it will be presumed that all professional visits made were deemed necessary and were properly made.

"There must not be too many consultations. The physician called in for consultation or to perform an operation may recover his fees from the patient, notwithstanding that the attending physician summoned him for his own benefit, and had arranged with the patient that he himself would pay." (This, of course, does not mean that the practitioner has a right thus to shift the burden of pay from his own shoulders.) "Where a medical man has attended as a friend, he cannot charge for his visit. Where a tariff of fees has been prepared and agreed to by the physicians of any locality, they are bound by it legally as far as the public are concerned (that is to say, they cannot charge more than the tariff rates), and morally as far as they themselves are concerned" (p. 5).

In these rules Dr. Ewell regards chiefly what conduct the courts of justice will sustain. It is evident that the Doctor is never entitled to run up his bill without any benefit to his patient; where there is no service rendered at all, there can be no claim to compensation. Still it is not necessary that actual benefit has resulted to the patient; it suffices for the claim to the fee that measures have been taken with a view to such benefit. Even when no physical advantage can reasonably be hoped for from the visit, the consolation it affords the patient and his friends may render those who are to bear the expense fully willing that it should be often repeated and, of course, charged on the bill. Provided care be taken that they understand the situation, no injustice is done them. "*Scienti et consentienti non fit injuria*" is a good moral maxim.

II. We have said that the rights conferred on the physician by the state are conditioned on his performing certain duties. He owes the same duties to his patients in virtue of the contract, explicit or implicit, that he makes with them by taking the case in hand. Under ordinary circumstances, neither the state nor the patients can oblige him to exercise his profession at all; but, if once he has taken a case in hand, he can be justly held not to abandon it till he has given his patient a fair opportunity of providing another attendant; even the fear of contagion cannot release him from that serious obligation.

The duties arising from the physician's twofold contract, with the state and with his patients, are chiefly as follows:

1. He must acquire and maintain sufficient knowledge of his profession for all such cases as are likely to come in his way. No Doctor has the right to attempt the management of a case of which he has not at least ordinary knowledge. In matters of special difficulty, he is obliged to use special prudence or ask for special consultation. The courts justly hold him responsible for any serious injury resulting from gross ignorance; in such cases they will condemn him for malpractice. I would here remark that, in an age in which the science of medicine is making such rapid progress, every Doctor is in duty bound to keep up with the improvements made in general practice, and in his own specialty if he has one.

2. A second duty is that of proper diligence in treating every single case. Many a patient suffers injury to health or even loses his life in consequence of a Doctor's neglect. Gross negligence is an offence that

makes him punishable by the court, if it results in serious injury. But even if such injury cannot be juridically proved, or has been accidentally averted, the moral wrong remains and is to be settled with the all-seeing Judge. Still, in ordinary ailments, no one is obliged to take more than ordinary trouble.

3. A third duty of the physician is to use only safe means in medical and surgical practice. He has no right to expose his patient to needless danger. What is to be thought of the use of such remedies as will either kill or cure? They cannot be used as long as safer remedies are available and capable of effecting a cure; for neither Doctor nor patient has a right to expose a human life to unnecessary risk. But when no safer remedies are going to effect a cure, then prudence itself dictates the employment of the only means to success. In such a case, however, the patient, or his parents or guardian, should, as a rule, be informed of the impending danger, so that they may give or refuse their consent if they please. For, next to God, the right to that life belongs to them rather than to the physician. The same duty of consulting their wishes exists when not life but the possible loss of a limb is at stake, or the bearing of uncommon sufferings. Moralists teach that a man is not obliged in conscience to submit to an extraordinarily painful or revolting operation even to save his life. Certainly, when the natural law leaves him at liberty, the physician cannot compel him to submit to his dictation; all he can do is to obtain his consent by moral persuasion.

4. As a consequence from the Doctor's duty to use only safe means it follows that he cannot experiment on his patients by the use of treatment of which he does not know the full power for good or evil. Nor is he excused from responsibility in this matter by the fact that the experiment thus made on one patient may be very useful to many others. His contract is with the one now under treatment, who is not willing, as a rule to be experimented upon for the benefit of others. And even if the patient should be willing, the Doctor cannot lawfully expose him to grievous danger unless it be the only

hope of preserving his life. This follows from the principle explained before, that human life belongs chiefly to God and not to man exclusively.

5. There are various kinds of medical treatment to which we can scarcely have recourse without exposing ourselves to serious evil consequences. Such is the use of cocaine, morphine, and even in special cases of alcohol. The drugs in themselves are useful, but they often lead to evil results. Now in the use of all such drugs as are apt to be beneficial in one way and injurious in another, we must ever be guided by the rules formerly explained concerning evil indirectly willed, or rather permitted to result, while good results are directly willed or intended. If the Doctor is satisfied that a dose of morphine or an application of cocaine will do more good than harm, he can, of course, prescribe or apply it. Still in such matters he must remember that the good effect is but temporary, while its pernicious consequences, especially when habits are thus contracted, are likely to be permanent and cumulative. Besides, the good results affect the body only, the evil often affect body and soul. Many a wreck in health and morals has been caused by imprudent recourse to dangerous treatment, where a little more patience and wisdom would have been equally efficient in curing the bodily ailment, without any deleterious consequences. If once a patient becomes a slave to the morphine or cocaine habit, the only cure is to cut off all the supply of the drug either at once or, at any rate, by daily diminution. To leave him free control of the poison is to co-operate in his self-destruction.

6. The sixth duty of a Doctor is of a different kind. There exists a tacit or implicit contract between him and his patients that he shall keep their secrets of which he becomes possessed in his professional capacity. It is always wrong wantonly to betray the secrets of others; but the Doctor is bound by a special duty to keep his professional secrets; and it is doubly wrong and disgraceful in him to make them known. For instance, if he has treated a case of sickness brought on by sinful excesses of any kind, he is

forbidden by the natural law to talk about it to such as have no special right to know the facts. Parents and guardians are usually entitled to be informed of their children's and their wards' wrong-doings, that they may take proper measures to prevent further evil. Besides, the Doctor is properly in their service; he is paid by them, and, therefore, his contract is with them rather than with the children. He can, therefore, prudently inform them of what is wrong, but he cannot inform others.

It is a debated question in Medical Jurisprudence whether the Doctor's professional knowledge of criminal acts should be privileged before the courts, so that he should not be forced to testify to a crime that he has learned from his patients while acting as their medical adviser. Dr. Ewell speaks thus on the subject (p. 2): "The medical witness should remember that, by the common law, a medical man has no privilege to avoid giving in evidence any statement made to him by a patient; but when called upon to do so in a court of justice, he is bound to disclose every communication, however private and confidential, which has been made to him by a patient while attending him in a professional capacity. By statute, however, in some of the United States, communications made by a patient to a physician when necessary to the treatment of a case are privileged; and the physician is either expressly forbidden or not obliged to reveal them. Such statutes exist in Arkansas, California, Indiana, Iowa, Ohio, Michigan, Minnesota, Missouri, Montana, New York, and Wisconsin. The seal upon the physician's lips is not even taken away by the patient's death. Such communications, however, must be of a lawful character and not against morality or public policy; hence, a consultation as to the means of procuring an abortion on another is not privileged, nor would be any similar conference held for the purpose of devising a crime or evading its consequences.

"A report of a medical official of an insurance company on the health of a party proposing to insure his life is not privileged from production; nor is the report of a surgeon of a railroad company as to the injuries sustained by a passenger in an accident, unless such report has been obtained with a view to impending litigation."

The practical rule for a Doctor's conscience on the subject of secrecy is, that he must keep his professional secrets with great fidelity, and not reveal them except in as far as he is compelled to do so by a court of justice acting within its legal power or competency. If so compelled, he can safely speak out; for his duty to his patient is understood to be dependent on his obedience to lawful authority.

As to the question of Jurisprudence whether the courts *ought* to treat the physician's official secrets as privileged, in the same way as they do a lawyer's secrets, this will depend on the further question whether the same reasons militate for the one as for the other. The lawyer's privilege is due to the anxiety of the state not to condemn an innocent man nor a guilty man beyond his deserts. To avert such evil, the accused party needs the assistance of a legal adviser who can guide him safely through the mazes and technicalities of the law, and, even should he be guilty, who can protect him against exaggerated charges and ward off unmerited degrees of punishment. Now, this can scarcely be accomplished unless the attorney for the defence learn from his client the entire truth of the facts. But the client could not safely give such information to his lawyer if the latter's professional secrets were not held sacred by the court of justice.

Can the same reasons or equivalent ones be urged in behalf of the physician? I do not see that they can. And I notice besides that, if he be excused from testifying against his patients, all their servants and attendants would seem to be entitled to the same privilege. Many persons, I think, labor here under a confusion of ideas; a Doctor is as sacredly bound to keep his patients' secrets as a lawyer is in regard to his clients, but it does not follow that the law cannot grant a privilege to the one and refuse the same to the other, for reasons which require it in the case of the lawyer and not in that of the Doctor.

III. Besides the rights and duties which arise for the physician from his contracts with the state and with his patients, there are other claims on his conscience, which proceed from his character as a man, a Christian, and a gentleman.

1. *As a man*, he is a member of the human family, not a stranger dwelling amid an alien race, but a brother among brothers. He cannot say, as did the first murderer, Cain, "Am I my brother's keeper?" But rather he must carry out the behest of the great Father of the human family: "God has given to each one care of his neighbor."

The maxim of Freemasons is that every member of that secret society must come to the assistance of every brother-mason in distress. But the law of nature and of nature's God is wider and nobler; it requires every man to assist every fellow-man in grievous need. The rich glutton at whose door lay Lazarus dying of want was bound, not by any human but by the higher law, to assist him; and it was for ignoring this duty that the soul was buried in hell, as the gentlest of teachers expresses it.

(*a*) As physicians, as men, you will have duties to the poor, who cannot pay you for your services; they are your fellow-men. Their bill will be paid in due time. He is their security who has said: "Whatsoever you have done to the least of these, you have done it unto Me." He may pay you in temporal blessings, or in still higher favors, if you do it for His sake; but pay He will, and that most liberally: "I will repay," says the Lord. The rule of charity for physicians is that they should willingly render to the poor for the love of God those professional services which they are wont to render to the rich for pecuniary compensation. While thus treating a poor patient they should be as careful and diligent as they would be for temporal reward; what is done for God should not be done in a slovenly fashion.

(*b*) In this connection of regard for the poor, allow me also to call your attention, gentlemen, to a point which students of medicine are apt to forget at times, and yet which both God and the world require you ever to bear in mind: it is the respect which every man owes to the mortal remains of a departed brother. I do not know that a people has ever been found, even among barbarians, who did not honor the bodies of their dead. For the good of humanity, dead bodies may at times be subjected to the dissecting-knife, but never to wanton indignities. Reason tells you to do by others as you wish to be done by, and Revelation adds its teaching about a future resurrection and glorification of that body of which the Apostle says that "it is sown in dishonor, but it shall rise in glory." Be men of science, but be not human ghouls. There is such a thing as retribution. But lately a former millionaire died in a poorhouse and left his body as a cadaver for medical students. We cannot afford to ignore the mysterious ways of Divine Justice. Ever handle human remains in a humane manner; and as soon as they have answered the purpose of science, see that they be decently interred, if possible.

2. There are other duties that you owe not as men but *as Christians*. All of us enjoy the blessings of Christian civilization, even those who are not Christians themselves. We are dealt with by others on Christian principles, and we ought to treat others in the same spirit. What duties does this impose?

(*a*) When your patients are in real danger of death, let them have a good chance to prepare properly for their all-important passage into eternity. Give them fair warning of their situation. Doctors and relations are often afraid of alarming the patients and thus injuring their health. But those who attend Catholic patients at least soon find out by experience that the graces and consolations of the Last Sacraments usually bring a peace of mind that benefits even the bodily health. In any case, the interests of the future life are too important to be ignored.

(*b*) For the same reason, the physician should not prescribe such doses of morphine or other anæsthetics as will render the patient unconscious at a time when he ought to be preparing to meet his Judge. This would be not kindness but cruelty. A little suffering more in this life may save much suffering in the next. If a Catholic priest, on being called to a patient's bedside, finds that the family's physician has been so inconsiderate, he cannot help protesting against employing such a man in Catholic families.

(*c*) If you attend a woman in childbirth, you may be asked by a Christian mother not to let her child die without Baptism. The vast majority of Christians believe that this sacrament is necessary to obtain supernatural happiness. The ceremony is easily performed: no harm can come of it, but immeasurable good for eternity. It should properly be performed by the clergy. But if this cannot be done, any man, woman, or child, even one not a Christian himself, can administer the sacrament. Every Doctor in a Christian land should understand how to do it, and do it with unerring accuracy. It were a disgrace for him to be ignorant of what even an ordinary child is expected to know. The ceremony is so simple; and yet, being an institution of Christ, no man can modify it to suit his notions; if what is done is not just what Christ appointed to be done, it will be of no avail. Notice, therefore, carefully every detail. You will take a little water, say a cupful, real water—cold or lukewarm, that matters not—you will slowly pour it on the head of the child, and, *while you do so*, you will say, "I baptize thee in the name of the Father, and of the Son, and of the Holy Ghost." That is all. Notice, you must say the words while the water is being poured on the child. For "I baptize" means "I wash"; pour, therefore, or wash while you say, "I wash." Should you hereafter wish to refresh your memories on this matter, you can do so by consulting the "Century Dictionary," which explains Baptism, and in particular Catholic Baptism, as "consisting essentially in the application of water to the person baptized by one having the intention of conferring the sacrament, and who pronounces at the same time the words, 'I baptize thee in the name of the Father, and of the Son, and of the Holy Ghost.'" If a cup of water given to the thirsty brings a blessing, how much more the giving of the water of salvation! Should it happen that the child is in danger of dying before delivery, it should be baptized in the womb provided it be at all possible to cause the water to reach or wash its body, projected upon it by any instrument whatever; but the water should flow over the body, not merely over the cyst enclosing it, for the cyst is no part of the child. Even if but an arm or other minor portion of the body is washed, the baptism is probably valid. If any doubt about the valid administration is left, the infant after delivery should be carefully baptized *under condition*, as it is called; that is, with the condition added that, if the former ceremony was validly conferred, there is no intention of giving a second baptism. For that would not be right; since the sacrament cannot be validly received more than once; it is a sacred initiation, but it were mockery to initiate one that is already initiated.

Should a physician be present when a pregnant woman has recently expired, and the child may still be living in the womb, it will be an easy and important task to perform the Cesarean section as soon as possible, and baptize the little one before it dies. In all this there is no money, but what is far more precious, the securing of eternal happiness. I add with great pleasure that many physicians are wont to comply with all these instructions most carefully, and even to instruct midwives and nurses in the best manner of rendering such services.

3. Lastly, we must consider the duties which a Doctor owes to others and to himself *as a gentleman.* It may not be easy to define what is meant by "a gentleman," and yet to some extent we all know it; we recognize a gentleman when we meet one, we pay him sincere homage in our hearts. We readily allow him to influence us and to guide us. We esteem him instinctively as a superior being, as we distinguish a precious stone from a common pebble; so we value a gentleman for precious qualities exhibited in

the beauty of his conduct. His conduct ever exhibits two characteristic marks: a proper degree of dignity or respect for self, and a proper degree of politeness or respect for others. Self-respect will not allow him to do anything which is considered vulgar, unmannerly, gross, rude, or selfish; he will avoid the two extremes, of self-neglect on the one hand and self-display on the other. His respect for others will make him treat all around him so as to make them feel comfortable in his presence; he will avoid whatever gives pain or causes embarrassment to even the lowest member of society.

Gentlemanliness has much to do with every one's success in life, and in particular with a Doctor's success. It is especially when sick that we are sensitive to everything displeasing in the conduct of others. It is not then the bold thinker or the extensive reader that is the acceptable visitor to the sick-room; but the gentlemanly consoler who always says the right thing at the right time, whose very eye expresses and whose countenance reflects the thought and sentiment most appropriate on the occasion.

There are most able physicians who are not gentlemen, and there are in the medical profession gentlemen who are rather poor physicians; but as a rule, I believe, the gentleman will thrive where the genius will starve. It is more or less the same in other professions. I know learned lawyers to-day who are far from prosperous, while men ten times their inferiors in learning are getting rich. I remember a most skilful physician, now no more on earth, who was a very genius in the science of medicine; but he was so filthy in his habits, he would so unceremoniously chew tobacco at all times, that many dreaded his visits, and would sooner have a man of less ability but gentler manners as their family physician.

Gentlemen, habits good and bad cannot be put on and off like a dress-coat; they are lasting qualities, the growth of years, the result of constant practice and self-denial or self-neglect. And, as I wish you success in life, allow me to conclude this lecture by recommending to you the assiduous cultivation of gentlemanly habits. Cultivate them now, while you are preparing for future labors. You wrong yourselves, and you insult your companions and your professors, when you neglect in their presence the conventionalities of polite society.

Uniting the external decorum of a gentleman with a thorough knowledge of your profession, and with what is still more important, the virtues of a conscientious man and a sincere Christian; ever true to the sound principles of morality which I have endeavored to explain and to inculcate in these lectures: you will be an honor to yourselves, an ornament to your noble profession, the glory and joy of your Alma Mater, a blessing to the community in which Providence will cast your lot as the dispensers of health and happiness and length of days to your fellow-men.

LECTURE VII.
THE NATURE OF INSANITY.

The subject of the present lecture, gentlemen, is "Insanity."

I. This subject belongs to a course of Medical Jurisprudence, because a physician who treats patients for insanity is liable, from time to time, to be cited before a court of law either as a witness or as an expert. His conduct in such cases is to be guided by the principles of natural and legal justice.

Various important cases at law turn upon the question of a person's soundness of mind; and frequently the medical expert has it in his power to furnish the court with more reliable information in this matter than any one else. At one time, the validity of a last will may be contested, and the possession of a fortune by one party or another may hinge on the question whether the testator at the time of making his will was in sufficient possession of his mental powers to perform an act of so much consequence.

At another time, interested parties may plead for or against the validity of a sale or other bargain made by a person of doubtful competency of mind; or a life-insurance company may be interested in ascertaining the mental condition of an applicant for membership; or it may be questioned whether the payment of an insurance policy is due to the family of a suicide, the doubt depending for solution on the sound or unsound condition of his mind at the moment of the fatal act. Again, there may be a real or pretended doubt whether a certain property-owner is so far demented as to be unfit to manage his estate; or whether he needs a guardian to take care of his person; or it may even seem necessary to confine him in a lunatic asylum. There may be objections raised to the mental soundness of a witness in a civil or a criminal suit; or, finally, a criminal prosecution will depend mainly on the sanity or insanity of the culprit at the moment when the crime was committed; as was the case with a Prendergast and a Guiteau.

You see, then, gentlemen, that important interests are dependent on the thorough and correct understanding of this matter; and therefore much responsibility rests upon the experts consulted in such cases: property, honor, liberty, nay, even life itself may be at stake.

That cases involving an insane condition of mind must be of frequent occurrence, both in the medical and in the legal professions, is apparent from the large and rapidly increasing amount of lunacy in our modern civilization. Wharton and Stillé's "Medical Jurisprudence" states (sec. 770, note) that in 1850 there was in Great Britain one lunatic to about one thousand persons; only thirty years later the Lunacy Commission of Great Britain reported one lunatic to 357 persons in England and Wales, that is, nearly three times as many. In New York there is one to 384 persons. It appears certain that its increase of late is out of all proportion to the increase of population; and even though I see reasons to distrust somewhat the figures quoted for England, enough is known to create serious alarm regarding the fruits of modern manners and customs on the minds of thousands. This fact makes the matter of insanity very important for the medical and the legal student.

II. Still it must be noted that the responsibility of deciding cases of lunacy does not rest chiefly with the medical expert. In cases of doubtful insanity the decision is to be given not by the Doctor but by the court of justice. Except on very special occasions, as when a physician is appointed on a committee or commission of inquiry, he appears before a court either as an ordinary witness, stating what facts have fallen under his personal observation; or as an expert, explaining the received opinion of medical men with regard to cases of a certain class. Even though he feels convinced that the culprit or the patient is as mad as a March hare, the physician cannot expect that his statement to that effect will be received as decisive. It is for the judge to instruct the jury what kind or degree of insanity will excuse a culprit from legal punishment, or will disqualify a person from testifying as a witness, or from being a party to a civil contract in certain cases; and it is for the jury to decide whether, in the case in hand, the fact of such insanity exists or not. In criminal cases, the jury pronounces on the double question, whether the accused did the act charged to him, and whether he has been juridically proved to have been accountable for the act under the laws as expounded by the judge.

1. To come to a decision on this double question, the jury might need to hear the facts stated which the physician has personally observed, and of which he is summoned to be a sworn witness. In such a situation all that is required of the Doctor is that he shall give a most faithful and intelligent account of the facts.

It would disgrace his standing in society if any fault could be found with his testimony; and, as a sworn witness, he is bound in conscience, like any other witness, to state the truth, the whole truth, and nothing but the truth. This is always the case when the purpose of the inquiry is the discovery of the sane or insane condition of a person's mind. But if the inquiry concerns the performance of the guilty act, the commission of the crime, many States of the Union, as explained before, consider the Doctor's professional secrets as privileged, just like those of the lawyer and the clergyman; i.e., the Doctor must not use against his patient any knowledge he has become possessed of while acting as his medical adviser.

2. When the physician appears before a court or commission as an expert, he is expected to give the views of the medical profession upon hypothetical cases resembling the one under examination, and the scientific reasons and authorities on which those views are advanced.

3. But here a considerable difficulty presents itself; it is so serious that, owing to it, the weight of the medical expert's testimony with judge and

jury is often much less than could reasonably be desired. The difficulty is to ascertain what really are the views of the medical profession on any given subject. Of course no individual Doctors can put themselves up as representing the convictions of the medical profession, nor can they always appeal to the unanimous agreement of their leading men. Leading physicians, unfortunately, are far from entertaining concordant views on many most vital questions. It is this want of agreement that has made the testimony of experts so powerless to sway the minds of judge and jury.

The medical profession has no organization through which it can pronounce judgment. In fact, many of its most conspicuous members have adopted principles at variance with the deepest convictions of mankind generally; such, for instance, are the followers of Darwin, Huxley, Maudsley, and similar agnostic and materialistic leaders of modern thought.

4. What still further diminishes the credit of medical experts is the fact that, both in civil and criminal trials, they are summoned either by the defence or by the prosecution, and are thus naturally selected, not on account of their thorough knowledge, but on account of their peculiar views known beforehand to the parties citing them. Thus their testimony is likely to be partial to either side, and is distrusted; at least it fails to command perfect confidence. The only way in which the prejudices thus created against the physician can be overcome is by his acquiring thorough knowledge of his specialty, and showing himself on all occasions to be as honorable and faithful as he is evidently experienced and intelligent.

5. The medical profession could be brought to be much more useful to society for the discovery of insanity if we could have here something like what exists in some parts of Germany. "The practice obtains there of requiring the medical faculty of each judicial district to appoint a special committee, to which questions of this kind are referred. This committee is examined directly by the court, and gives testimony somewhat in the same way, and with the same effect, as would a common-law court when

reporting its judgment in a feigned issue from chancery, or as would assessors called upon under the canon law to state, in proceedings under the law, what is the secular law of the land on the pending question" (Wharton and Stillé, sec. 274).

The matter of introducing some such practice into this country has been agitated of late, and may by and by lead to beneficial results. Dr. Shrady has taken steps to promote this object by striving to have a law enacted by the New York legislature providing for the regulation of expert medical testimony in jury trials. According to his plan, once such a commission has been established, the court is to send the medical issue to these experts, just as it sends other issues to special juries to be decided. The regular petit jury will then decide only upon the facts constituting the crime.

This would do away with special pleas of insanity before a jury that knows little or nothing about the nature of the disease, and whose sympathies may readily be worked upon by shrewd lawyers to render a verdict of acquittal.

As things are now, the medical expert, summoned to testify in a case of contested sanity or insanity of mind, ought to rise above minor considerations, and promote the cause of justice, by giving all the valuable information that his profession enables him to acquire on the very difficult subject of mental unsoundness.

6. For this purpose, he must be skilled in three departments of science.

(a) In *law*—sufficiently to understand what are considered by the courts as characteristic marks of an insane mind, and what amount of sanity the courts require to hold a culprit responsible for his crime or a contract valid in its effects.

(b) In *psychology*—to such an extent that the expert witness can speak analytically and correctly as to the properties and actions of the human mind.

(*c*) In *medicine*—so far as concerns the treatment of the insane, and the understanding of their peculiarities, so as to reason from them by induction to the real condition of the client's or patient's mind.

But the main requisite for an expert witness is to understand clearly in what insanity properly consists, and how far it ought to excuse an insane man from bearing the consequences of his acts.

III. This two-fold knowledge is obtained by the psychological study of insanity, on which study we are now to enter, and it is the principal point in this whole matter.

Insanity means a want of soundness; he is insane whose mind is not sound, but is deranged, and therefore, like a machine out of order, it cannot properly perform its specific task, namely, to know the truth of things. An insane man cannot judge rightly.

1. Insanity takes various forms, which may be reduced to two kinds, with the doubtful addition of a third kind, namely, moral insanity, of which we shall speak in our next lecture.

The first kind consists in the total want or gross torpor of mental activity. When there is a total, or nearly total, eclipse of the intellect, the disease is called *idiocy*, the state of an idiot. When there is an abnormally low grade of the reasoning power, it is styled *imbecility*. The failure or decay of reason in old age is called *dotage*.

The second kind of insanity is called *illusional* or *delusional*. In it the intellect is not impotent; on the contrary, it is often unusually active; but its action is abnormal, its conclusions are false. Not that it reasons illogically or draws conclusions which are not contained in the premises. Very keen logicians may be demented. Their unsoundness arises from the fact that they reason from false premises; and they get their false premises from their diseased imaginations, whose vagaries they take for realities.

2. Here a difficulty presents itself, which we must explain at once, namely, how can there be unsoundness of mind at all? Is not the intellect of

man a simple power, and his soul a simple being? How can a simple being become deranged? Can that which has no parts become disarranged, disorganized? I answer, the soul is a simple being, its intellect is a spiritual faculty; and therefore we never say that the *soul* is insane, nor should we say that the *intellect* is insane or diseased; but we say that the *mind* is deranged or insane; the mind comprises more than the intellect; it designates the intellect together with those lower powers that supply the materials for our thought, the chief of which is the imagination. Now the imagination is an organic faculty: it works in and by a bodily organism, which is the brain. Therefore, when the brain is not in a normal condition, the action of the imagination may be disordered. And the intellect or understanding of the spiritual soul is so closely united in its action and its very being with the organic body that the two ever act conjointly, like the two wheels of a vehicle. If one wheel breaks down, the other is thrown out of gear. Thus it is readily understood that mental unsoundness is an affection of the brain, a bodily disease, which may often be relieved and even cured by bodily remedies, by the use of drugs or wholesome food, healthy exercise, fresh air, and all that benefits the nervous system.

Pathologically considered, the nerves may be too excited or too sluggish and torpid; and we have as the result two subdivisions of mental insanity—*mania* and *melancholia*. The differences between these two are very striking; as they proceed from opposite causes they produce opposite effects, and, therefore, they betray themselves by very different manifestations; but in one point the two agree, and with this point precisely we are concerned, because in it lies the essence of mental insanity, namely, that both produce a disordered action of the imagination.

3. The manner in which the imagination co-operates in mental action is this. It presents to the intellect the materials from which that power forms its ideas. When we see, feel, hear, taste, or smell anything by our bodily senses, our imagination takes note of the object perceived by forming a

brain-picture of it which is called a *phantasm*. I do not mean to say that it forms a photographic picture of the object; for there can be no photographing taste or smell or feeling; but it forms an image of some kind which it presents to the intellect. This power at once proceeds to form, not a brain-picture, but an intellectual or abstract image of the object presented. For instance, you see this book, and at once you, in some mysterious way which has never yet been explained, impress some image of it on your brain. That you do so is clear from the fact that the image remains when the book is withdrawn. That material image or brain-picture is the *phantasm*. It is not an *idea*, though it is often improperly so called. But your intellect forms to itself an idea of a book; that is, you know what is meant by a book. You distinguish between the mere form of a book and the book itself. Your idea of a book is a universal idea, which stands for any book, no matter of what shape or size. Every phantasm, or brain-picture, is a representation which presents its object as having a definite shape or size, while your idea of a book ignores any shape or size. And yet, when your intellect conceives a book, your imagination will picture some particular form of book. If your brain became so affected by disease as to be unfit for the formation and retention of the proper phantasms, then your intellect either would not work at all or it would work abnormally; your mind would then be insane.

4. Now, in an infant the brain is still too soft and imperfect to form the proper phantasms from which the intellect is to elaborate its ideas. A false school of psychology would say that the infant's brain cannot yet *ideate*; but that is incorrect language. No brain can ideate or form ideas; an idea is an intellectual or mind image, not a brain image; it is an abstract and universal image, and matter cannot represent but what is concrete and individual. Only a simple and spiritual being, the rational soul, can form ideas. Nevertheless our soul, in its present state of substantial union with our body, is extrinsically dependent on the body; to form ideas it needs to have the sensible object presented to it by a phantasm or brain-picture.

Now, a child born blind and deaf, and thus having its mind, as it were, cut off from communication with the outer world, could scarcely form the necessary phantasms, because the clogged senses could not supply proper materials for them; such a child would, therefore, be apt to remain idiotic. And even in children whose outer senses are sound the brain or the nervous system may be too imperfect to allow of its forming proper phantasms. In this torpor of the mind then consists the first kind of mental unsoundness, that of *idiocy*, or its milder form *imbecility*. In old age, and in peculiar diseases, the worn-out system may return to a second childhood, then called *dementia* or *dotage*. The existence of such species of insanity is not difficult to discover.

5. The second and more common form of insanity, and that which it is often difficult to discover and pronounce upon with certainty, is that which I have called *delusional* or *illusional*. Its characteristic trait, its very essence, lies in this, that the insane man mistakes what he imagines for what is real; and he cannot be made to distinguish between imagination and reality, though the difference is obvious to an intellect in its normal state.

In this connection, it is well to point out a distinction, not always observed, but useful to explain the workings of an insane mind, between *illusions, hallucinations*, and *delusions*.

(*a*) An *illusion* is properly a deception arising from a mistake in sense-perception; as when a half-drunken man sees two posts where there is only one. He has a picture of the post in each eye, and his brain is too much disturbed to refer the two pictures to the same object. In this case the cause of the mistake is subjective. A *mirage* offers another instance of a sense-illusion; but in it the cause is objective.

(*b*) A *hallucination* is a creation of the fancy mistaken for a reality. The deception may be but momentary, as when Macbeth is stealing on tiptoe to the chamber of his guest to murder him. His mind is disturbed by the imagination of the horrid deed he is about to perpetrate. He thinks he sees a dagger in the air, and he says: "Is this a dagger that I see before me, its handle towards my hand? Come, let me clutch thee. I hold thee not, and yet I see thee still; and on thy dudgeon gouts of blood, which was not so before." But Macbeth, upon a moment's reflection, sees it is all imagination. "There's no such thing," he exclaims. He is not insane, though deceived for a while.

(*c*) A *delusion*, on the contrary, is a permanent deception, whether it results from an illusion or a hallucination, it matters not; as a fact, it almost always originates in hallucinations. The deluded man clings to his imaginings; you cannot talk them out of his head. Such is the case of an inebriate who suffers from *mania a potu*, or "the horrors;" he sees snakes and demons, he thinks, and persists in his error. Such also is a fixed idea not arrived at by faulty reasoning, but come unbidden and proof against all reasoning and evidence. Thus an insane man may be convinced, solely by his imagination, that he is poisoned or pursued or conspired against.

6. This delusion constitutes the essence of mental insanity, which therefore is often called delusional insanity. It may be chronic, i.e., of long continuance, or it may be temporary, acute. For the time being, the effects are the same. Perhaps any man may, at times, be for a moment thrown off his guard, and mistake a fancy for a reality; this does not constitute lunacy. But when the error is so firmly held in the mind's grasp that nothing can dislodge it thence, then the mind is deranged in its special sphere of action, which consists in knowing the real from the unreal; the mind is then insane.

You notice, gentlemen, that I speak of the mind as grasping the error, and I suppose it to do so independently of the free will's command. But when the error is voluntary; when a man clings to it simply because he loves it; when he hugs a delusion to his heart, this shows not mental but moral obliquity; it is not insanity but self-deception, and it is by no means of rare occurrence. In a well-reasoned article on "The Metaphysics of Insanity," written by Mr. James M. Wilcox and printed in the "American

Catholic Quarterly Review" for January, 1878, some very severe and no less true strictures are made upon the readiness of a vast multitude of people to practise this wilful self-deception. "Self," he writes (p. 54), "is the prolific origin of such errors; and so indulgent are we to its faults that we try secretly to hide them even from our own eyes, mostly with success; and where success is not perfect, we make a second effort to hide the imperfection. Repeated efforts of this kind, from which we but half turn away, are crowned in the end, and we soon forget what successful hypocrites we have been. Our numerous passions, the complexities of our desires, the tenacity of their grasp, and the pleasant gentleness of its touch explain an infinity of temptations followed by wilful successes in blindness, all of which are nothing less than guilty acts of self-deception."

7. It oftens[**] happens in real insanity that mental derangement manifests itself upon one error or one group of errors only, while for all the rest the patient appears to be quite rational. Such a man is called a *monomaniac*. But he is truly an insane man; for the essence of insanity is in him. It is usually found that a monomaniac will, sooner or later, exhibit signs of mental unsoundness on other matters as well; and even while he has given no such signs, it still remains true that a mind cannot be trusted, but has something radically unsound about it, if it is really unhinged at any point at all.

But then you must be very careful not to confound monomania with eccentricity. The distinction is as important as it is real. *Eccentricity* is a conscious aberration from the common course of life; it consists in peculiarities in reasoning, words, and actions, which are wilfully indulged, in defiance of popular sentiment. The eccentric man knows that he is eccentric; he is willing to be so, and to take the consequences; but he is not insane.

As this matter is of frequent occurrence before the courts of justice, and the validity of last wills in particular often depends on the view that judges and expert witnesses take of it, I think it well to refer the earnest student for further information to Wharton's and Stillé's "Medical Jurisprudence," in the volume on "Mental Unsoundness and Psychological Law;" in particular to secs. 29, 38, 39, 40.

8. We must now return to the consideration of the manner in which the disturbance of the brain may affect the mind. The brain is a storehouse of records of things formerly noted there by the imagination, either as the results of sense perception or of arbitrary combinations of phantasms; it is a library of facts and fancies. And these are not single, but grouped together, so that when one is stirred it will arouse others as well. When the brain is affected, whether by an acute or a chronic derangement, its images may become so disordered that records of mere imaginations get mixed up with records of real perceptions in inextricable confusion. You may have had occasion to notice the process in the case of a man who is becoming intoxicated and then passes on to *mania* or *delirium tremens*: he gradually proceeds to mix up brain-pictures with realities, and after a while he speaks and acts like a very crazy man. He is in a kind of dream; his imaginations are wild and disconnected, his language is incoherent.

The delirium arising from violent fevers, for instance from typhoid fever, is very similar to that arising from the excessive use of intoxicants and narcotics; similar in these respects; that the mania is only temporary, and that the exciting cause is not altogether unknown.

The *bacilli* of the infection, like the alcohol, the opium, the morphine, or other drugs, are accountable for the disordered action of the brain. But I do not pretend to know, nor do medical writers generally pretend to understand, *how* the poison, or whatever causes the disease, gets to affect the brain. Does it do so directly, or by means of the alteration it causes in the whole nervous system or in the blood? We do not know; nor does it matter for the purposes of Medical Jurisprudence.

IV. The questions with which the courts of justice, the lawyers, and the expert witnesses are concerned are these: Is the man really insane? Or was he insane at a given time when he performed a certain civil or criminal act? Is he now, or was he then, so far controlled by his mental unsoundness as to be incapable of acting like a rational being accountable for his actions? Even if he is now, or was then, a monomaniac, can the deed in question be traceable to his monomania as to its real cause?

1. When we know that a man is suffering from a fever, or has been drinking to excess, or has been addicted to the use of morphine, opium, cocaine or to similar deplorable practices, it is then easy enough to conclude from this that he is not in his right senses; knowing the cause, we can fairly estimate the effect. But in many cases of delusional insanity the cause is hidden; neither pulse nor other medical test betrays it. Whether the mind is sane or not is then to be found out from the man's words and actions; and these may be affected for a purpose: he may play the fool to escape punishment.

2. Phrenologists have pretended that the peculiarities of a person's mind could be known by the conformation of his brain, and even by the elevations and depressions of the skull. But brain and skull do not always correspond with sufficient closeness; and besides, Sir William Hamilton has shown conclusively, I believe, that phrenology is quackery; its principles are not scientific and its observations not reliable. He points out, among other errors, that while women as a class are more religiously inclined than men, what phrenologists call the bump of reverence, an important element in religious sentiment, is generally more developed in men than in women, and is often most conspicuous in reckless criminals.

Nor is it at all certain that a lunatic's brain, if it could be examined with a microscope while he is alive, would exhibit the marks of any disorder to the eye of the observer. It is stated by Dr. Storer that the results show that "insanity may exist without structural changes of the brain, and that structural changes in the brain may exist without insanity." Dr. Bell, of the Somerville Asylum, says that "the autopsies of the insane generally present no lesion of the brain." Dr. Bucknil maintains that "the brains of the insane appear to be certainly not more liable than those of others to various incidental affections." Nor has the microscope discovered in the demented any exudation or addition to the stroma of the brain, or any change in size, shape, or proportional number of its cells. Dr. Storer concludes: "It is thus seen not merely that there is no direct correspondence between the exterior of the skull and mental integrity, any more than between the exterior of the skull and the shape and consistence of its contents" (Wharton and Stillé, "Mental Unsoundness," sec. 323). In the cases of insanity among women, the causes are largely to be found in derangement of their productive organs, and are to be met by special local treatment (ib.).

It does happen, however, at times, that the brain itself is diseased, *idiopathically* diseased, as it is technically called; but at other times it is merely affected by *sympathy* with some other organ that is physically deranged. A physical cause there is for all mental insanity, and that physical cause determines its kind of mania or melancholia, its duration, its chances of a perfect cure. But what that cause is in a given case is often very hard if not impossible to determine. Besides natural and inherited predispositions —some taint of derangement in the family, often betrayed by fits of epilepsy, hysterics, etc.—exciting causes are usually traceable. Every form of disease may bring on sympathetic affection of the brain when the circumstances for such affection are favorable.

But while affirming that the disease usually arises in the body, and even frequently in parts far removed from the brain, we must not deny nor ignore the fact that intellectual and protracted worry, or sudden and violent grief, can also be the direct cause of disturbance in the brain. For the brain is the organ not of the imagination alone, which is put to an unhealthy strain by excessive mental labor, but probably also of the passions, whose emotions when excessive may cause even permanent lesion. Hence mental insanity may and does often arise from ill-subdued passions.

The knowledge of all this may enable the physician to remove the exciting cause or to mitigate its influence; it may also aid expert witnesses, judges, lawyers, and jurymen to ascertain the main fact with which the courts are concerned, namely, the presence or absence of mental insanity at the time of a given civil or criminal action.

V. Supposing then that, in the case before the court, the fact of insanity is established, the next question of Jurisprudence to determine is this: How far and why ought such unsoundness of mind to exclude responsibility for deliberate acts?

It is a clear principle of reason that no man can justly be blamed or punished for doing what he cannot help doing; now an insane man cannot help judging wrong at times; he cannot then justly be blamed for acting on his mistaken judgments. If he invincibly judges an act to be morally good whereas it is morally bad, no matter how criminal the act may be—say the killing of his own father or child—if he commits the deed with the full conviction that he is doing right, he cannot be blamed or punished for committing that awful crime.

The principle then is clear that an insane man is not to be held responsible to God or man for his insane acts. For the root and reason of our responsibility for an act lies in the fact that we do the deed of our own free choice; knowing its moral nature, being masters of our own free will, so that, if we do one act in preference to another, we wilfully take upon ourselves the consequences of this preference as far as we can know or suspect them.

If we do what we are firmly convinced is right, just, worthy of a man, we deserve praise; if we do what we are convinced or suspect is wrong, unjust, unworthy of a man, we deserve blame and punishment. But an insane man may do the most unjust act, and yet feel invincibly convinced that it is just; he cannot then be held responsible for doing it, because the root of responsibility is then wanting.

I do not, however, maintain that one who is insane on any one point is thereby made irresponsible for all his actions. If he does what he thinks to be wrong, he acts against the dictates of his conscience, he deserves punishment from God; and if he violates a just law of the land, and it can be proved that his deed proceeded from a bad will, he may be punished by the civil courts as well, even though he is insane on other points. For instance, if a young man were to have a crazy notion that his father disliked him, that he is often in various ways unjust to him, and if, in consequence of this insane conviction, he were to attempt his father's life, he should be punished for the criminal act; because, even according to the way he views the matter, he could not be justified in killing his father for such a reason. It were different if he insanely imagined that his father was in the act of killing him, and that he could not escape death but by killing his father first; for then he could plead the right of self-defence against an unjust aggressor, as he foolishly imagines his father to be.

The conclusion then from all this explanation is that an insane man should not be held responsible for a deed which he insanely thinks to be right; but he is responsible for all his other acts.

In our next lecture we shall consider more fully the treatment of the insane by the civil and criminal tribunals.

LECTURE VIII.
THE LEGAL ASPECTS OF INSANITY.

In our last lecture, gentlemen, we considered the nature and causes of delusional insanity. We saw that its essence lies in mistaking imaginations for realities with a firmness of conviction which no argument to the contrary can shake. The reasoning of the insane man may be logically faultless, we said, but he reasons from false premises supplied to him by the phantasms of a diseased imagination. The cause of the disease I showed to lie in an abnormal action of the brain, which is the storehouse of the phantasms or brain-pictures. And this abnormal action may itself proceed either from a local lesion of the brain, or from a sympathetic affection due to indisposition in other parts of the human body. I finished by examining the responsibility of an insane man for his actions, and arrived at this practical conclusion, that a victim of delusional insanity should not be held responsible for any acts which he insanely thinks right, but should be held responsible for all his other human acts.

I. This teaching of psychological and ethical science is to-day the received rule of action followed by the courts of justice in England and the United States. Sound philosophy and positive law are in perfect agreement on this subject. But it was not so a hundred years ago. It is wonderful to us now how strange and erroneous were the views of insanity formerly entertained by English jurists. For instance, when, in 1723, Arnold was tried for shooting at Lord Onslow, the instruction given to the court was that, for one to be exempt from punishment in such a case, "it must be a man that is totally deprived of his understanding and does not know what he is doing, no more than an infant, than a brute or a wild beast." On such a theory, very few lunatics indeed would be acquitted; few ever are so totally demented.

The first jurist that pointed out the true test of insanity was Lord Erskine, who, in 1800, when Hudfield was tried for shooting at the king, delivered a celebrated speech, in which he maintained that the real test of insanity was in delusion: if delusion existed the man was insane; else, he was not insane. The deluded man, he said, might reason with admirable logic from his false principles; he was nevertheless demented if he mistook his imaginations for realities, and did so irresistibly and persistently.

Erskine's test has been, from that time on, followed in the courts of England. But you will notice, on careful consideration, gentlemen, that while the principle is correct so far as it goes, it does not go far enough to cover all cases of disputed responsibility. It will apply, indeed, to all cases of total insanity, that is, when the delusion existing in a lunatic's mind affects a variety of subjects; then his premises are never reliable, and therefore he cannot be held accountable for any of his acts.

But what if his insanity is partial only, if he is a monomaniac, deranged on one point and sound in mind on all other matters? This was not clearly understood till about the middle of the present century. In order to secure uniform views and action on this important matter, the British Parliament, in 1843, proposed various questions to the judges, with a request that they would agree upon and report answers. This investigation, and in fact the whole history of English legislation on insanity, is briefly and yet clearly explained in an article of Rev. Walter Hill, S.J., which appeared in the "American Catholic Quarterly Review" for January, 1880. The first question was: What was the law respecting the crime of one who is partially deluded but not insane in other respects, when he commits what he knows to be a crime in order to redress some wrong or obtain some public benefit? The answer was that such a one, even though insane, is to be punished for the crime which he knew he was committing.

To another of those questions the judges answered, that a person partially insane was to be treated *as if the facts were just what he imagined them to be,* as if his delusions were realities. His conduct was to be judged by his own premises. This was accepted as law by England, and is the law now both there and here, and, I suppose, throughout the civilized world. Now, these are exactly the conclusions about an insane man's responsibility which we had arrived at before, reasoning from psychological and ethical first principles.

It is therefore for the consequences of an insane delusion only that a man is not responsible before the inward court of conscience and the outward courts of justice.

But the case is altogether different when the error is not the result of insane delusion. When a man, sane or partially insane, has reasoned himself into a false opinion or conviction, not the result of his insanity, that the crime he is going to commit is justifiable, such conviction being his own free act does not exempt him from punishment. This was the precise point on which turned the celebrated case of Guiteau, the murderer of President Garfield. His trial before the Supreme Court, District of Columbia, December, 1882, was one of the most interesting that have ever occurred in this country or elsewhere in connection with the plea of insanity. In his very able and exhaustive instructions to the jury on that occasion, Judge Cox states the rule that is to guide the jury in these words: "It has been argued with great force on the part of the defendant that there are a great many things in his conduct which could never be expected of a sane man, and which are only explainable on the theory of insanity. The very extravagance of his expectations in connection with this deed—that he would be protected by the men he was to benefit, would be applauded by the whole country when his motives were made known—has been dwelt upon as the strongest evidence of unsoundness. Whether this and other strange things in his career are really indicative of partial insanity, or can be accounted for by ignorance of men, exaggerated egotism, or perverted moral sense, might be a question of difficulty. And difficulties of this kind you might find very perplexing if you were compelled to determine the question of insanity generally, without any rule for your guidance.

"But the only safe rule for you is to direct your reflections to the one question which is the test of criminal responsibility, and which has been so often repeated to you, viz., whether, whatever may have been the prisoner's singularities and eccentricities, he possessed the mental capacity, at the time the act was committed, to know that it was wrong, or was deprived of that capacity by mental disease."

What furnished the clearest proof, gentlemen, that Guiteau's opinion concerning the expediency of killing the President resulted not from an insane delusion but from his own reasoning is contained in a paper which he had himself drawn up to justify the murder.

It is an address to the American people, published on June 16, in which he says: "I conceived the idea of removing the President four weeks ago; not a soul knew my purpose. I conceived the idea myself and kept it to myself. I read the newspapers carefully, for and against the Administration, and gradually the conviction dawned on me that the President's removal was a political necessity, because he proved a traitor to the men that made him, and thereby imperilled the life of the Republic." Again he says: "Ingratitude is the basest of crimes. That the President under the manipulation of the Secretary of State has been guilty of the basest ingratitude to the Stalwarts, admits of no denial. The express purpose of the President has been to crush Senator Grant and Senator Conkling, and thereby open the way for his renomination in 1884. In the President's madness he has wrecked the once grand old Republican Party, and *for this he dies.*—This is not murder. It is a political necessity. It will make my friend, Arthur, President, and save the Republic," etc.

When instructing the jury, Judge Cox told them clearly that, if they found, from all the testimony presented, that the culprit had been led to commit the murder by an insane delusion, they were to acquit him; but that reasoning one's self into an opinion or conviction was not acting upon an insane delusion. "When men reason," he said, "the law requires them to reason correctly, as far as their practical duties are concerned. When they have the capacity to distinguish between right and wrong, they are bound to do it. Opinions, properly so called, that is, beliefs resulting from reasoning, reflection, or examination of evidence, afford no protection against the penal consequences of crime." On this precise point of the question then the verdict was to depend.

But to understand this matter thoroughly there remains one more important point to notice in the instructions of Judge Cox. It relates to the question on whom rests the burden of proof regarding the existence of insanity in the culprit. Is the prosecution bound to prove that insanity did not influence the crime? Or is the defence to prove that it did? And, in case neither party can prove its point to a certainty, so that the jury remains in doubt as to the existence or the influence of insanity in the crime, is the doubt to weigh in favor of the culprit or against him? The judge, after a careful exposition of the conflicting views on this subject by different courts, and after weighing their respective claims, favors the opinion which holds that "the sanity of the accused is just as much a part of the case of the prosecution as the homicide itself, and just as much an element in the crime of murder, the only difference being that, as the law presumes every one to be sane, it is not necessary for the government to produce affirmative proof of the sanity; but that, if the jury have a reasonable doubt of the sanity, they are just as much bound to acquit as if they entertain a reasonable doubt of the commission of the homicide by the accused."

But the jury, enlightened by the lucid instructions of the court, were convinced that Guiteau had not been led to commit the murder by an insane delusion, but by his own reasoning and his own free will, and that, therefore, he was to bear the consequences of his own deliberate choice. Their verdict was "guilty," and the political crank was hanged.

II. We have now done with the study of mental or delusional insanity; it remains for us to speak of moral insanity. Of late years, the legal and medical professions have been much divided upon the question whether there exists a disease which may properly be called moral, emotional, or affective insanity, and which can justly be pleaded as an excuse from legal responsibility.

Dr. Pritchard, and later on, Dr. Maudsley, with very many followers, have maintained the existence of such a disease, and have claimed that, even when it is not accompanied by any delusion, it ought, nevertheless, to free a man from all punishment for crimes committed under its influence. Moral insanity consists, they say, in a perversion of the will, which by this disease is deprived of its liberty, so that the morally insane man does what he knows to be wrong, but cannot help doing it. And they claim that therefore he cannot be blamed nor punished for the crime he thus commits, although he commits it knowingly and willingly.

But I absolutely deny that such a state of insanity is possible. It is against those clear principles of psychology and ethics which are not only speculatively evident, but practically necessary to maintain the fabric of human society. I do not deny that there exists an emotional insanity of another kind, which I will explain further on, but not an insanity of the will, as they understand it, which would excuse a man from the consequences of his wilful acts. Upon this subject Dr. Chipley justly remarks: "If one is born with all the emotional endowments of our nature, but destitute of understanding, his irresponsibility is unquestionable. The same is true when the faculties of the understanding are perverted, impaired, or destroyed by disease.

"In every aspect in which man's accountability is viewed, we arrive at the same point that its sole basis is the existence and soundness of the intellectual powers. Those wonderful endowments which so eminently distinguish man from other animals, which enable him to discriminate between good and evil, right and wrong, and to choose the one and avoid the other; or in the language of Judge Robertson, he is accountable because he has the light of reason 'to guide him in the pathway of duty, and a *free* and *rational* presiding will to enable him to keep that way in defiance of all passion and temptation.'

"If then accountability is a structure erected solely on the intellectual power, must it not remain unshaken so long as its foundation is sound and unbroken? Is it not illogical to set out with the fundamental proposition, that man is made responsible for his acts only because he is gifted with an understanding and then arrive at the conclusion that he may become irresponsible without the impairment or disease of any of its powers?" (Wharton and Stillé, "Mental Unsoundness," p. 170.)

Gentlemen, let me give you a specimen of the false reasoning used in support of their theory by those who believe in the insanity of the will. "It would be as rational," says one of their leading writers in this country, "to punish a schoolboy whose antics and grimaces, the result of chorea [St. Vitus' dance], are a source of laughter and distraction to his schoolmates, as to inflict punishment upon the insane criminal who, knowing the difference between right and wrong, has it not in his power to execute that which his judgment dictates. One is under the dominant influence of insanity of the *muscles*, the other is under the influence of insanity of the *will*. To punish one would be as cruel as to punish the other." This is indeed a very illogical argument. The reason why we do not blame the boy is because his will is not in it; he moves against his will. The reason why we blame the other is because his will is in it; he does what he wills to do.

The will being a spiritual power can no more be diseased than can the intellect. But as the imagination, an organic power, can be disorganized by an affection of the brain, and by delusion deceive the intellect, thus producing mental insanity, similarly I fully admit that a man's passions, which are also organic powers, common to us and to brute animals, can become disordered by bodily disease; and the passions, when excited, will strive to drag along the consent of the will, as we all experience. A man whose passions are abnormally influenced by bodily disease, so that he is constantly inclined to act very unreasonably, may well be called morally insane. Such a state of insanity is not a rare occurrence, and there is no objection to denominate it emotional, affective, or moral insanity.

But in such a disease the will remains free; if a man does what he knows to be wrong and criminal, he then sees reasons for not doing it; and in this lies the root of his liberty. For seeing himself drawn in one direction by one motive and in another by another motive, he is not determined in his choice but by the act of his free will. A merely organic faculty must be determined by the stronger attraction, as is the case with brutes; but a spiritual faculty, as our will is, acts freely in choosing between two opposing motives of action. This is the philosophical or psychological explanation: and I am well pleased to find that here again, as in the matter of mental insanity, the courts of England and the leading courts of the United States follow the sound teachings of philosophy.

The nearest advance I know of, that has been made towards the recognition of this moral insanity as a total bar to responsibility, was made in 1864 by the court of appeals in Kentucky, and again in 1869 under the same presiding Judge Robertson. But Chief Justice Williams rebukes this strange ruling in most emphatic language. He says: "In all the vague, uncertain, intangible, and undefined theories of the most impractical metaphysician in psychology or moral insanity, no court of last resort in England or America, so far as has been brought to our knowledge, ever before announced such a startling, irresponsible, and dangerous proposition of law, as that laid down in the inferior court. For, if this be law, then no longer is there any responsibility for homicide, unless it be perpetrated in calm, cool, considerate condition of mind.

"What is this proposition if compressed into a single sentence? that, if his intellect was unimpaired and he knew it was forbidden both by human and moral laws; yet if at the *instant* of the act his will was subordinated by any uncontrollable passion or emotion causing him to do the act, it was moral insanity, and they ought to find for the plaintiff?... If so, then the more violent the passion and desperate the deed, the more secure from punishment will be the perpetrator of homicide or other crimes.... The doctrine of moral insanity, ever dangerous as it is to the citizen's life, and pregnant as it is with evils to society, has but little or no application to this case. Too uncertain and intangible for the practical consideration of juries, and unsafe in the hands of even the most learned and astute jurist, it should never be resorted to for exemption from responsibility save on the most irrefragable evidence, developing unquestionable testimony of that morbid or diseased condition of the affections or passions, so as to control and overpower or subordinate the will before the act complained of" (ib., p. 172).

You will notice, gentlemen, that Chief Justice Williams does not deny the existence of every kind of moral insanity. As I explained before, not the will but the passions may really be diseased or insane, and they may prompt the lunatic to commit very unreasonable and even criminal acts. When the impulse of a passion is violent, so that a man is carried along by it before he has had time to reflect on the criminal nature of his act, or at least before he could do so calmly and deliberately, the courts readily recognize such passion as a partial excuse: murder thus committed in a moment of strong provocation becomes manslaughter, not murder in the proper sense of the word. It is not justifiable; but yet it is far less criminal and less severely punished than when committed in cold blood, or, as the law terms it, with malice prepense or aforethought. This practice of our courts is right and highly reasonable, because on such occasions the will of the culprit is partly overpowered, or deprived of freedom.

It is a matter of much discussion among jurists whether a passion can ever be so violent as to overpower the will *absolutely*, so as to deprive it of all freedom at the moment. If it can, then the culprit should be totally acquitted for doing what he could not help doing. In several States of the Union, such an invincible impulse has been recognized by the courts of justice, and men have been acquitted for acting on what was supposed to be an invincible impulse to commit crime; the courts considered this as an extreme form of moral insanity.

I have shown above that on sound principles of philosophy the will can never be compelled to do wrong; at most it could be said that, in the cases just referred to, the will was not in the act. Now this, I suppose, is the case in hydrophobia or *rabies*, in which terrible disease the biting of the sufferer appears to be spasmodic, not voluntary. It is very doubtful whether such excuse can be substantiated in what is called moral insanity.

The courts of England and the leading authorities in the United States have never departed from this correct rule, that a man is accountable, to some extent at least, for whatever he does willingly and without the influence of delusion.

Moral insanity thus understood, as a derangement of the passions lessening a man's full mastery of himself, but not destroying it altogether, assumes various forms. There are kleptomania, or an abnormal impulse to steal; pyromania, an impulse to set things on fire; dipsomania, or an abnormal fondness for intoxicants; nymphomania, or the tyranny of lustful passions; homicidal mania, or a craving to commit murder; etc. In all these the nature of the disease is the same, it would appear. The imagination seizes the pleasure vividly, yet, it is claimed, without delusion: and the passion, owing to organic disorder, is abnormally excitable. The organic derangement is supposed to be in the brain. For the human brain, a masterpiece of the Creator's wisdom, is now generally believed to consist of various portions which are the organs of the passions, of motive power and the phantasms, erroneously called ideation. Hence it is easy to understand how it may happen that one portion is diseased while the other parts are in a normal condition. And on the other hand it thus appears very probable also that a brain partially diseased is liable to be soon affected in the other parts as well. Hence we may suspect that moral insanity is likely to bring on delusional insanity, and *vice versa*. In fact, I find that a medical expert of note, who had for many years taught that moral insanity was quite a distinct disease and separate from mental insanity, has in his old age changed his mind to some extent on this subject. "Of late years," says Dr. Bauduy, of St. Louis, in his learned work on "Diseases of the Nervous System," "I have believed, notwithstanding the doctrine of Pritchard, that a careful study of moral insanity will enable us to detect some evidence, although, it must be confessed, often very feeble, of mental weakening. Even the classic cases of Pritchard," he adds, "who first defined the so-called moral insanity, when carefully examined, will confirm this statement" (p. 227). Usually, as the same Dr. Bauduy explains, those who are morally insane are at least on the high road to mental insanity (p. 228). Moral insanity is known to exist when there is a sudden change of character which can have no other source than bodily disease; as when a most honest man becomes of a sudden an habitual thief, a decent man openly profane, a miser becomes extravagantly liberal, an affectionate father a very tyrant to his children, without any traceable causes for such transformation. The disease is made more manifest if such a sudden change is preceded by certain physical conditions, such as epilepsy, hereditary taint, suicidal attempts, "the insane temperament," as it is called, and other influences which are to be taken into consideration.

If ever you be summoned, gentlemen, to testify or pronounce on a person's insane condition, let me give you one piece of advice which may spare you much unpleasantness: be unusually cautious of what you say. If you appear as an expert or a witness, and you make a mistake unfavorable to the patient, he will be your enemy for life; even he may at times recover damages for libel. If he is really crazy, he may be all the more dangerous. Do your duty, of course, as an honest man must always do; but do it very prudently.

Dr. Bauduy is very emphatic on the assertion that moral insanity is not moral depravity. He is perfectly right; yet we must not forget that moral depravity is often screened before the courts by the plea of insanity. When a man of bad antecedents commits a crime, and is known to have been sane just before and after the deed, he ought not to be excused on the plea that he may have been insane at the moment when he committed the act; there is no reason for such a plea. And with the victims of kleptomania, dipsomania, and other moral manias, it is well known that a sound whipping will often stop the nuisance. The rod for the juvenile offender, and the whipping-post for adults, would cure many a moral leper and be a strong protection for society at large, especially if applied before bad habits freely indulged have demoralized the person beyond the usual limits. All of us have our passions; they are an essential part of our nature and even an indispensable part. But they should be controlled by reason and will, whereas they are often indulged with guilty weakness. They are much strengthened by indulgence, especially in those predisposed to certain vices by hereditary transmission. No doubt some children have worse passions to contend against than others. It is still worse if, at the same time, their surroundings are unfavorable to virtue; and this is a constant source of increase to the criminal classes.

Wise statesmen will study the ways in which temptations to vice may be diminished; but it is mistaken mercy and dangerous to the community to spare the guilty when once they have committed criminal acts. If ever the principle were admitted in our courts of justice that the possible existence of mental insanity ought to protect a culprit from punishment, crime would soon increase tenfold both in the sane and in the insane. Both classes must be kept impressed with the conviction that the law rules supreme and will not tolerate the destruction of public safety. Your profession, gentlemen, in this matter as in many others, by its sound views on Jurisprudence and Ethics, is one of the strongest bulwarks of the common good.

LECTURE IX.
HYPNOTISM AND THE BORDER-LAND OF SCIENCE.

In this last lecture of our course I propose to make a brief excursion with you into the border-land of science, a region chiefly occupied by imposture and superstition. To show there is such a territory, we have only to name a few of its inhabitants, such as mesmerism, animal magnetism, odylism, hypnotism, mind-reading, faith-cures, clairvoyance, spiritism, including table-rapping, spirit-rapping, most of which have been used in connection with medicine. I do not maintain that all of these are mere vagaries, empty shadows, without the least reality, mere ghosts and hobgoblins, mere phantoms of the heat-oppressed brain, or cunning devices of impostors to deceive a gullible crowd of the ignorant public. Yet most of these are such beyond a doubt, and as such are totally unworthy of our attention.

Medicine is a science; it deals with undoubted facts and certain principles, and with theories in so far as they are supported by well-ascertained realities. The border-land of which I speak presents to our investigation few certain facts. It is chiefly the domain of imposture. Charlatans and showmen and medical quacks call things facts that are not facts. Among all the inhabitants of the shadowy region that I have enumerated, there is only one considered to-day by the science of medicine as worthy of its attention. It is hypnotism. As its first origin is connected with the history of mesmerism, and the latter, though itself a phantom, has been used as the chief patron of all other phantoms, I will premise a few words about mesmerism itself.

I. Mesmer was born about 1733, studied in Vienna and there became a doctor of medicine in 1766. Soon after, he began to speculate upon the curative powers of the magnet, and claimed to have discovered the existence of a force in man similar to magnetism and the source of strong influence on the human body.

In 1775 he published an account of the medical powers of this animal magnetism, which from his name was afterward called *mesmerism*. Paris was then the centre of attraction for scientific discoverers and pretenders. Thither Mesmer betook himself and there he soon created a lively sensation by the exhibition of mesmeric trances, some of which were accompanied by clairvoyance—that is, the power of seeing objects concealed from the eyes. He was also supposed to work some inexplicable cures.

The secret of his art he could not be induced to reveal even for the sum of 340,000 livres, which was offered him in compensation. People began to doubt whether he had a real secret, or whether he was a rank impostor. A royal commission was appointed to examine into the matter. Our Benjamin Franklin, then in Paris, was one of the commissioners. Their report was unfavorable. They found no proof of the existence of a fluid such as animal magnetism, and thought that all that was not imposture could be accounted for by the power of imagination. In a secret report they pointed out very strongly the dangers likely to arise from this unhealthy stimulus to the imagination. Their verdict does honor to their learning and their common-sense. Mesmer left Paris, and he died in obscurity in 1815.

But his pretended discovery did not die with him. It was a mine of resources to charlatans and impostors generally. There were strange effects produced, and at the sight of the inexplicable men lose their wits. The gullible public wondered, restless minds experimented, and many pondered thoughtfully on facts, most of which were not facts at all. But after eliminating all the elements of imposture and exaggeration there seemed to remain a residue of phenomena that were strange and unaccountable.

II. THEORY OF HYPNOTISM.

About 1840 the vaunted claims of the many clairvoyants were exposed before the French Academy of Medicine, which passed a resolution rejecting mesmerism altogether as unworthy of notice on the part of scientific men. The theory of a mesmeric fluid, until then the only one advanced, had evidently to be abandoned. Science with all its tests could find no such cause of the results produced. But in 1842 an English physician, Dr. James Braid, hit upon a more plausible theory. He conjectured that the actions of the mesmeric subject could be explained without a fluid by the suggestion of phantasms to him on the part of the mesmerizer. Dr. Carpenter, then a great authority, defended his theory; but the medical branch of the British Association disdained to consider the matter. Dr. Braid thought the mesmeric trance was only a state of somnambulism artificially brought about, and he coined the word *hypnotism* to indicate the artificial sleep. Other attempts to promote the cause of hypnotism were made in the United States and other lands, but no very definite or scientific results were reached until 1878, when the celebrated Prof. Charcot and others made its nature and possibilities the subject of a thorough study and abundant experimentation at the Paris hospital of La Salpétrière and in other places. At present it is admitted by distinguished medical scientists that hypnotism is a reality, capable of being utilized for important purposes. Many effects have been demonstrated to be produced by it as real as any ordinary phenomena of nature. But on the explanation of their causes there hangs still a cloud of obscurity.

The Paris School of Doctors attribute the effects to physical causes, chief among which are diseases of the nerves. Those of Nancy trace the phenomena to a psychical source, namely, to suggestion—that is, action on the subject through his imagination excited by words, signs, or in any other manner. This appears to be, in the main, the theory of Dr. Braid vindicated by modern science. Probably enough, both schools are right in their way, the suggestions not taking effect except where nervous affections have prepared the way. The beneficial results claimed for hypnotism by the scientific men who have made its study a specialty are chiefly as follows:

III. BENEFITS OF HYPNOTISM.

1. It acts as a temporary sedative, quieting the excited nerves of the patient. It was thus employed, for instance, on an old woman who was near her death, and who had not been able to make necessary preparations for that important event, being beside herself with nervous agitation. She obtained by this means a calm condition for some seven or eight hours. Hypnotism was for her like the visit of a good angel from heaven.

2. It is used as an anæsthetic in place of chloroform, which in many cases cannot be applied without great danger to health, or even life. Thus perfect insensibility may be procured and long continued, allowing sometimes of the performance of protracted surgical operations that would otherwise be almost impossible.

3. At other times it is employed as a mere pain-killer without depriving the patient of consciousness, so that the hurt is felt indeed, but not attended with keen suffering.

4. It is claimed that the skilful application of hypnotism can at times not only alleviate the pain of an injury, but even cure nervous affections more or less permanently, removing, for instance, the defect of stammering.

5. There are not wanting cases in which even moral improvements are claimed to be produced, at least in the removing of bad habits, such as drunkenness. If hypnotism can cure intoxication permanently, or even for a season, it deserves to be encouraged. Yet even then it must be used with great caution, for there may be very evil consequences resulting from its

use. To realize fully the dangers and the evils attendant upon hypnotism you must understand the three stages through which the patient is made to pass —those of lethargy, catalepsy, and somnambulism.

IV. DANGEROUS TREATMENT.

Each of these is a disease in itself, and thus it is seen at once that a treatment which employs diseases as its means of cure must be of a dangerous kind. After the patient has been hypnotized by any of the various processes—the chief are mesmeric passes of the hypnotizer's hands, his eyes fixed into the eyes of his subject, or the latter's on an object so held as to strain his eyes—the first stage of hypnotism is obtained, that of lethargy. In the lethargic state, the subject appears to be sunk in a deep sleep; his body is perfectly helpless; the limbs hang down slackly, and when raised fall heavily into the same position. In this condition all the striated or voluntary muscles react on mechanical excitement. Without an accurate knowledge of anatomy, much harm may be done by the experiment.

The second stage is that of catalepsy, certainly not a healthy condition to be in. Its grand feature is a plastic immobility by which the subject maintains all the attitudes given to his body and limbs, but with this peculiarity, that the limbs and features act in unison. Join the hands of the patient as if in devout prayer, and his countenance assumes a devout expression; clench his fist, and anger is depicted in his features.

The third stage is that of somnambulism. The skin is now insensible to pain, but excessive keenness is manifested in the sight, hearing, smell, and muscular sense. Here the impostor can play off his pretended clairvoyance or second sight; for the subject will discover objects hidden from sight by the sense of smell and other senses affected with abnormal power. The somnambulist will now exhibit the utmost sensibility to suggestions made to him by the hypnotizer, so that he seems to be almost entirely controlled by the influence of the latter's will. This is what chiefly favored the early theory that a mesmeric fluid emanated from the mesmerizer by means of which he could act in his subject as he pleased. The experiment by suggestions seems to succeed best with hysterical patients, which fact confirms the morbid character of the hypnotic trance.

V. FIELD FOR A SCIENTIST.

If any distinguished scientist or Doctor who can afford it wishes to make a special study of hypnotism, which is still so imperfectly understood, he may render a valuable service to humanity, and in particular to the science of medicine. But if any ordinary physician asked my advice about devoting attention to this pursuit. I would emphatically tell him, "Leave it alone: you are not likely to derive real benefit from it, and you are very likely to inspire your clients with distrust of you when they see you deal with matters which have deserved a bad name on account of the charlatanism and the superstitious abuses usually connected with them." This is not my opinion alone, but also that of distinguished writers on the subject.

VI. OBJECTIONS TO HYPNOTISM.

When there is question of hypnotic séances or exhibitions such as are designed to feed the morbid cravings of the public for what is mysterious and sensational, I would call special attention to the following objections against such practices.

1. Medical authorities maintain that it requires at least as much knowledge of therapeutics to use hypnotism safely as it does for the general practice of medicine, and requires of a physician who engages in it a more thorough mastery of his profession than many other branches of the healing art, and therefore that it is as objectionable to allow non-professionals to deal with hypnotism as it would be to allow medical practice promiscuously to all persons without a Doctor's diploma. In fact, in Russia, Prussia, and Denmark none but licensed physicians can lawfully practise hypnotism. Aside from a variety of accidents which may result to the subject hypnotized from the ignorance of physiology in the hypnotizer, there is this

general injury sustained, that even strong subjects frequently experimented upon contract a disposition to be readily thrown into any of the three morbid states of the mesmeric trance. All these states are real diseases and are allied to hysteria, epilepsy, and a whole family of nervous troubles, any one of which is sufficient to make a patient very miserable for life, and even to lead him to an early grave.

2. The moralist has still stronger objections against the use of hypnotism, except when it is used as a means to most important results. He maintains that one of the greatest evils that can befall a man is the weakening of his will-power; this leaves him a victim to the cravings of his lower appetites. Now the frequent surrender of one's will to the control of another is said (very reasonably, it would seem) to bring on a weakening of the will or self-control. We see this exemplified in the habitual drunkard. He loses will-power to such an extent that he can scarcely keep his most solemn promises or withstand the slightest temptations. There is a very serious question asked by the moralist upon another resemblance of an hypnotic subject to a drunkard. He asks whether any man has a right for the amusement perhaps of the curious lookers-on to forfeit for awhile his manhood, or the highest privilege of his manhood—his powers of intellect and free-will. He admits that we do so daily in our sleep. But then he argues that sleep is a necessity of our nature directly intended by the Creator, a normal part of human life. Besides it is a necessary means for the renewal of our strength, and on the plea of necessity the moralist may admit the use of hypnotism when it is needed for the cure of bodily diseases. But for the mere amusement of spectators he maintains that it is wrong for a man thus to resign his human dignity, as it would be wrong for him to get drunk for the amusement of lookers-on. Still, in this latter case the evil would be greater, for in drunkenness there is contained a lower degradation, inasmuch as the baser passions are then left without all control, and are apt to become exceedingly vile in their licentious condition. The hypnotic subject has at

least the mind and will of the hypnotizer to direct him. Here, however, appears the need of another caution, namely, that the hypnotizer should be known to be a virtuous man; else the evil that he can do to his subject, as is readily seen, may be even worse than that resulting from a fit of drunkenness. And as men who occupy even respectable positions may yet be vile at heart, it is very desirable for prudence' sake to have no one hypnotized in private without the presence of a parent, close relative, or some other party, who will see to it that nothing improper be suggested during the trance. For the scenes gone through during the hypnotic state, though not remembered by the subject upon his return to consciousness, are apt to recur to him afterwards like a dream, showing that they have left traces behind them.

3. Legal writers and lawyers have serious charges against hypnotism. This practice, they maintain, if publicly exhibited to old and young, begets dangerous cravings for sensational experiments. Turning away men's attention from the sober realities and duties of social life, it prompts them to pursue the unnatural and abnormal. It was this craving that in less enlightened ages led men to the superstitious practice of astrology and witchcraft. At present it leads to such vagaries and unchristian and often immoral practices as are connected with spiritism, faith-cures, mind-reading, and similar foolish or criminal or at least dangerous experimentations which dive into the dark recesses found in the border-land of the preternatural. The atmosphere of that region is morally unhealthy and should be barred off by the guardians of public morals.

The most common objection of legal writers is directed against the various crimes to which hypnotism is apt to lead men of criminal propensities. They point to the statements of Dr. Luys, a respectable authority on hypnotism, who says: "A patient under the influence of hypnotism can be made to swallow poison, to inhale noxious gases. He can be led to make a manual gift of property, even to sign a promissory note or bill, or any kind of contract." Indeed, how can notaries or witnesses suspect any fraud when even the Doctor needs all his experience and all his skill to avoid falling into error? In criminal matters a man under suggestion can bring false accusations and earnestly maintain that he has taken part in some horrible crime.

VII. FURTHER EXPLANATION OF HYPNOTISM.

After considering the objections to the use, or rather abuse, of hypnotism, I may add some further explanation of hypnotism itself—of its nature so far as it is known to science. Science has ascertained the reality of the phenomena and facts—not single facts only, scattered here and there, but groups of facts uniformly obedient to certain laws of nature. It has not yet discovered the exact cause or causes of all these phenomena, but it gives plausible explanations of them, both in the physical theory of the Paris School and in the psychical theory of the Nancy School of Physicians. Science has discarded the original theory of a mesmeric fluid as the cause of these phenomena, just as it has discarded the formerly supposed fluids of electricity and magnetism. Of electricity the "Century Dictionary" says: "A name denoting the cause of an important class of phenomena of attraction and repulsion, chemical decomposition, and so on, or, collectively, these phenomena themselves." The true nature of electricity is as yet not all understood, but it is not, as it was formerly supposed to be, of the nature of a fluid. Similarly we may define hypnotism as the collection of peculiar phenomena of a trance or sleep artificially induced, or the induced trance or sleep itself.

The true cause of these phenomena is not yet understood, but there is no apparent reason for attributing them to a special fluid; they seem to be peculiar ways of acting, belonging to man's physical powers when his nerves are in an abnormal condition. By laying down these definite statements we gain the advantage that we isolate hypnotism from the frauds and empty shades, from the ghosts and hobgoblins with which it used to be associated in the border-region which we have undertaken to explore. Science deals with well-ascertained facts. Now of mesmerism, animal magnetism, and its kindred, odylism, we have seen that we have no reliable facts. We have done with those unsubstantial shades. But of hypnotism we have well-known facts, and we have shown it to be placed on a scientific basis.

VIII. SCIENCE DREADS ERROR.

Of clairvoyance, mind-reading, palmistry, spiritual science cures we have no certain facts, but we have many impostures connected with them. If ever we get real and undoubted facts proved to be connected with them, we ought to examine them with care. Science is not afraid of any portion of nature; all it dreads is ignorance, and what is worse, error. Error with regard to facts may be committed in two ways—by admitting as facts what are not facts, and by denying facts. Now, there are facts certain and well ascertained, numerous and widely known, connected with some other portions of the border-land of science that we have not yet looked into, though I have mentioned their names. He who would assert that spiritism, table-turning, spirit-rapping, and so on are mere idle talk, sheer impostures, is not well read in the literature of the present day. By denying all reality to these phenomena he strays as far from the truth as if he allowed himself to believe mere fabrications. They are not impositions, but they are worse; they are superstitions. By superstitions I mean here the practice of producing results which cannot possibly proceed from the powers of nature, and which could not without absurdity be attributed to the interference of the Creator or His good angels.

Some persons strenuously object to introducing any reference to God into scientific works. Science consists in tracing known effects to their true causes. If there were no God, He could not be a true cause and it would be unscientific to introduce His agency. But if there is a God and He acts in the world which He has made, we must take His actions into account when we study His works. Some say, "I do not believe in a God." That may be, but that does not prove that there is no God. Belief is a man's wilful and fine acceptance of what is proposed to him on the authority of some one else. Students have most of their knowledge on the authority of their professors and other men of learning. If a medical student would say, "I do not believe in microbes nor in contagion by disease germs," that would not kill the germs nor protect him against contagion. Nor would it show his superior wisdom, but rather his extravagant conceit and ignorance. So with those who believe not in God.

There are others who believe not in the existence of devils or fallen angels. That is not so bad; but yet they must remember that their refusal to believe in devils does not prove that there are none. The greatest enemies of science are those who blindly maintain false statements and false principles of knowledge. Let us look for the truth in every investigation. Even Huxley, in the midst of his attacks on dogmatic religion, protests also against dogmatic infidelity. Science, he says, is as little atheistic as it is materialistic. All this must be remembered chiefly when we undertake to explore, as we are now doing, the unknown region which we have called the border-land of science. There we find many strange phenomena, and we are trying to discover their true nature and true causes. If we can explain some of them by natural causes, as by the powers of the imagination when it is in an abnormal or hypnotic state, very well, let us explain them. But let us not rashly conclude that all other phenomena can be thus explained. Do not reason this way, as some writers have done: "Some effects," they say, "were formerly attributed to witchcraft or deviltry and can now be explained by hypnotism. Therefore all other mysterious effects can also be thus explained. Therefore there is not and never was such a thing as witchcraft or deviltry. So, too, some events often reputed miraculous can be explained by natural causes, therefore no miracle has ever happened." That is the reasoning of rash and ignorant men, and not of scientific minds. It does not follow from the fact that God usually works by natural causes, that He cannot on special occasions and for very important reasons show His hand, as it were, and act so manifestly against the course of nature as to show us that it is He who is at work and He wants us to mind Him. History furnishes many instances of this kind.

IX. CREDENTIALS OF CHRIST.

Least of all have Christians a right to deny this, and we must remember that the civilized world is Christian, almost entirely. Christians believe in the reliability of the Bible, and in it we are constantly informed of countless miracles in various ages. If all these accounts are false, then Christianity is a vast imposture. Christ appealed to them as to His credentials in His mission to the world. "If you do not believe Me," He said, "believe My works, for they give testimony of Me. The blind see; the lame walk; the dead are raised to life." If He spoke falsely, He was a deceiver; if He worked those marvels by hypnotism, or any other natural cause, He was an impostor. There is no middle way. Either by working true miracles He proved Himself to be what He claimed to be, the Son of God, or He was the most bold and detestable impostor that has ever appeared on earth. This no Christian can suppose, this no historian would admit; therefore, we must grant that He worked miracles, and miracles are realities to be taken into account by the writers of history, and scientific workers must not sneer at them.

X. DEVILTRY.

Scientific men in their investigations need not expect to come into contact with miracles; but they may and do find in the border-land of science facts which reveal the agency of intellectual beings distinct from men, and too vulgar in their manifestation to be confounded with God or His blessed angels. Such agents in the book of the Scriptures are called devils, and intercourse with them is styled superstition, seeking their assistance is magic or witchcraft, and consulting them is divination or fortune-telling. All these practices are directly and strictly forbidden in the Scriptures, and yet they are commonly enough in use in our own day to procure effects that gratify the curiosity of such, especially, as have no settled belief in supernatural religion.

Some of these effects are connected with bodily cures and thus are of interest to physicians. For instance, spiritualistic mediums, whether connecting their practices with magnetism or not, though entirely ignorant of medicine, are at times able to state the exact bodily indisposition of sick persons living at a great distance, put into communication with them by holding some object belonging to them. They will indicate the seat of the disorder, its nature and progress, its complications. They propose simple and efficacious remedies, using not infrequently technical terms which are certainly unknown to them before. They manifest the thoughts of others, reveal family secrets, answer questions put in languages of which they know nothing. To deny facts attested by thousands of witnesses of various nations belonging to various religious denominations or professing no religion whatever, is not the spirit of science. It it estimated that 100,000 spiritist books and pamphlets are sold yearly in the United States alone. It is certain that much, very much imposture is mixed up with many undeniable facts, but that does not dispose of the real facts mixed up with the impostures. Tyndall once caught an ill-starred spiritualistic impostor at his juggling. He concluded that all other spiritists were impostors. The world now laughs at him for his foolish reasoning.

Of course, I do not suppose that spiritism is mainly employed in such matters as would directly interest the physician. It has grown into a system of religion and morals, very peculiar and at variance with the Christian religion, a system rather resembling the religion of Buddha, with its reincarnations and transmigrations of souls while struggling after eternal after-progress. This is fully and clearly explained in an article on "Spiritism in its True Character" in the English publication called "The Month," for September, 1892. But with this phase of it we are not now concerned. As to the facts, it is enough to remark that spiritists claim a following of 20,000,000. Suppose there are only one-half that number. 10,000,000 people are not readily deceived about matters of their daily observation, for their meetings or séances consist chiefly of those manifestations which others call impostures.

Their adherents are chiefly among the educated classes, I believe. Certainly they include multitudes of doctors, lawyers, professors, scientists, magistrates, clergymen, close students, keen intellects, even such men as Alfred Russell Wallace, Profs. Morgan, Marley, Challis, William Carpenter, and Edward Cox. If one has still lingering doubts on this matter let him read the four learned articles written by my predecessor in this chair of Medical Jurisprudence, Rev. James F. Hoeffer, S.J., the former president of Creighton University. They are found in the "American Catholic Quarterly Review" for 1882 and 1883.

What must we think of the nature of spiritism, with its spirit-rappings, table-turning, spirit-apparitions, and so on? Can such of the facts as are not impostures and realities be explained by the laws of nature, the powers of material agents and of men? All that could possibly be done by the most skilled scientists, by the most determined materialists who believe neither in God nor demon, as well as by the most conscientious Christians, has only served to demonstrate to perfect evidence that effects are produced which can no more be attributed to natural agency than speech and design can be attributed to a piece of wood. One principle of science throws much light on the nature of all those performances, namely, that every effect must have a proportionate cause. When the effect shows knowledge and design, the cause must be intelligent. Now many of these marvels evidently show knowledge and design; therefore the cause is certainly intelligent.

A table cannot understand and answer questions; it cannot move at a person's bidding. A medium cannot speak in a language he has never learned, nor know the secret ailment of a patient far away, nor prescribe the proper remedies without knowledge of medicine. Therefore these effects, when they really exist, are due to intelligent agents, agents distinct from the persons visibly present; invisible agents, therefore, spirits of another world.

Who are these agents? God and His good angels cannot work these wretched marvels, the food of a morbid curiosity, nor could they put themselves at the disposal of impious men to be marched out as monkeys on the stage. The spirits which are made to appear at the séances are degraded spirits. Spiritualists themselves tell us they are lying spirits. Those lying spirits say they are the souls of the departed, but who can believe their testimony if they are lying spirits, as they are acknowledged to be? This whole combination of imposture and superstition is simply the revival in a modern dress of a very ancient deception of mankind by playing on men's craving for the marvellous. Many imagine these are recent discoveries, peculiar to this age of progress. Why? This spirit-writing is and has been for centuries extensively practised in benighted pagan China, while even Africans and Hindoos are great adepts at table-turning. It is simply the revival of ancient witchcraft, which Simon Magus practised in St. Peter's time; which flourished in Ephesus while St. Paul was preaching the Gospel there. It is more ancient still. These were the abominations for which God commissioned the Jews in Moses' time to exterminate the Canaanites and the other inhabitants of the Promised Land. In the Book of Moses called Deuteronomy, or Second Law, admitted as divine by Catholics, Protestants, and Jews alike, we have this fact very emphatically proclaimed by the Lord. He says: "When thou art come into the land which the Lord thy God shall give thee, beware lest thou have a mind to imitate the abominations of those nations; neither let there be found among you any one that ... consulteth soothsayers, or observeth dreams and omens, neither let there be any wizard, nor charmer, nor any one that consulteth pythonic spirits, or fortune-tellers, or that seeketh the truth from the dead."

Is not this just what spiritualists pretend to do? Many may call it only trifling and play. The Lord does not. The Scriptures continue: "For the Lord abhorreth all these things, and for these abominations He will destroy them at thy coming." I certainly do not mean to say that all that passes for spiritualism is thus downright deviltry to-day, nor was it so in pagan times. Much imposture was mixed with it. The oracles of the pagan gods and goddesses were not all the work of the pythonic spirits. Much was craft of the priests of idols; and yet all were abominations before the Lord, on account of the share that Satan took in the deceptions.

What must be the attitude of the scientific man towards all such matters? It should be an attitude of hostility and opposition. Science should frown down all imposture and superstition. Medicine in particular, intended to be one of the choicest blessings of God to man, should not degrade its noble profession by pandering to a vulgar greed for morbid excitement. Not only will you personally keep aloof from all that is allied to quackery and imposture, but in after-life your powerful influence for good will be most efficient in guarding others against such evils, and even perhaps in withdrawing from such associations those who have already got entangled in dangerous snares. At all events the enlightened views you shall have formed to yourselves on all such impostures and impieties will be a power for good in the social circle in which your mental superiority and your moral integrity will make you safe guides for your fellow-men.

www.ingramcontent.com/pod-product-compliance
Lightning Source LLC
Chambersburg PA
CBHW081819200326
41597CB00023B/4304